Believing Today

Jew and Christian in Conversation

Leon Klenicki
and
Richard John Neuhaus

WILLIAM B. EERDMANS PUBLISHING COMPANY
GRAND RAPIDS, MICHIGAN

Library of Congress Cataloging-in-Publication Data

Klenicki, Leon.
Believing today: a dialogue/by Leon Klenicki and
Richard John Neuhaus.
p.   cm.
ISBN 0-8028-0313-X
1. Judaism—Relations—Christianity—1945- 2. Christianity and
other religions—Judaism. I. Neuhaus, Richard John. II. Title.
BM535.K554   1989
261.2'6—dc19   88-13934
CIP

In Memoriam

ABRAHAM JOSHUA HESCHEL

JACQUES MARITAIN

Preface

Christian-Jewish dialogue in its current form has been around for approximately fifty years. There are significant parts of the Jewish and Christian communities for which it is still quite new. Indeed, there are Christians and Jews who have not participated in the dialogue at all, and who are profoundly suspicious of it. But it is fair to say that most of our churches and synagogues, at least here in the United States, have been touched by the dialogue in one way or another. And we would like to think it has been a touch of blessing for Jews and Christians alike.

The two of us are deeply grateful for the dialogue. And yet the reader would not be mistaken if he or she detected in the conversation that follows a note of dissatisfaction with it as well. So much of the Jewish-Christian dialogue and the materials that flow from it are marked by a strained courtesy, an eagerness not to offend. A great deal of it is also stilted and thus very official in tone. No doubt both of us have contributed over the years to conferences and studies that are excessively formal. We hope that those efforts too, whatever their weaknesses, have served an important purpose. This little book, however, is something quite different.

It really is a conversation and is intended to be entirely informal and entirely candid. Here and there it may even hurt, touching on sore points that more formal exchanges might seek to avoid. We hope it will be evident that this is a conversation between friends. More important to the reader, we hope it will be evident that this is a conversation between believers. Believers in the same God? To respond to that question is precisely one of the chief purposes of the conversation.

At the risk of being misunderstood, we should say at the outset that our primary aim in publishing this book is not to advance the Christian-Jewish dialogue. Our primary aim is to advance the argument that, if Jews and Christians who are "believers today" are more faithfully Jewish and more faithfully Christian, the dialogue will take care of itself. Put differently, the dialogue is not something that is in addition to being Jewish and Christian; it is an integral part of being Jewish and Christian today. The dialogue is not a hobbyhorse for "people who happen to be interested in that sort of thing." We are called to this enterprise by God, and it is his enterprise before it is ours. The dialogue is most fully served by our becoming more fully Christian and more fully Jewish. It is served by our disagreements as well as by our agreements. In sum, we think that the late Abraham Joshua Heschel put it well when he said, "Interfaith dialogue begins with faith."

We trust the reader will take from this little book a better understanding of the differences and similarities, the divisive arguments and unifying beliefs, between Christians and Jews. But, most of all, we hope the reader will be provoked to reflect anew on the adventure that is "believing today."

Leon Klenicki
Richard John Neuhaus

Believing Today

Beginning with Faith

Neuhaus: We aren't quite sure where we'll be going, but we thought we might begin with the question of what is meant by Jewish-Christian dialogue—the history of it, the problems associated with it, where we think it ought to go. Perhaps, Leon, you could get us started on that.

Klenicki: We might start by defining the word "dialogue" itself. The word has been used and misused in the interfaith relationship, and I think it warrants some examination. My first definition would be that dialogue is an encounter of partners. Dialogue is an exchange—a physical exchange, encountering the other as a person in front of us, and a spiritual exchange, understanding the other as a person of God. It is an exchange of two entities, in this case Judaism and Christianity. Dialogue is not only a relationship of words, signs, and gestures, but also a mixture of past experiences, present realities, and the possibility for a future.

In dialogue as an encounter, we should introduce ourselves, present ourselves, as we are—that is, as subjects of God committed to long-standing traditions and to rebuilding that tradition in our present situation in the world. We are trying together to analyze the meaning of our present interchange of words—and I use that phrase "interchange of words" deliberately;

such an interchange is a prelude to a deeper, meaningful reality.

My concern is that sometimes in dialogue we are not projecting our unity as people of God, but rather projecting our divisions: problems of the past, painful memories—especially for us Jews in the Western world—or prejudice, essentially the Christian teaching of contempt, which started with the Church Fathers' view that, after Jesus, the Jewish people had no role in God's design because they denied Jesus as the Messiah. This contempt was expressed in theology as well as in social discrimination.

Neuhaus: Here we are in agreement. Dialogue has to be much more than simply intergroup relations or the resolution of difficulties at the level of conflicting group interests. That is why we've thought of titling this little book *Believing Today*. It is, as you say, a matter of *believers* encountering one another, with the acknowledgment that we do not always believe the same things. But the very encounter assumes, in an odd but important way, a measure of unity that is already there.

There is a *logos*, a word of God, that has anticipated us and that makes significant encounter possible. Put differently, the dialogue must be understood as a trialogue. A true dialogue, at least between believers, always includes not merely another party but the primary party, who is the God in whom we believe. And so, in our explorations, we encounter one another—in a way that we cannot fully comprehend but that we are prayerfully conscious of—in God. The late Abraham Joshua Heschel was fond of saying, "Interfaith dialogue begins with faith." If that is forgotten, the dialogue really does descend into being no more than an exercise in intergroup relations.

Klenicki: We are partners in the presence of God. The

rabbinic tradition, which later was incorporated into the New Testament, stresses that when two or three persons are together praying or studying the Torah, they are surrounded by God: the *Shekinah*, the presence of God, is among them. And this is what dialogue should essentially be: founded in faith, as you pointed out so rightly. The Hebrew word for faith, *emunah*, hints at the reality of being under God. The term is related to another word that we use constantly in our prayers, in both the church and the synagogue: *amen*—accepting God. By having faith, by exercising faith, we accept God and accept the obligation of bringing God into our reality and the reality of our people. So a dialogue is an exchange of word and experience—not with the idea of reaching a syncretism, but rather of sharing the presence of God.

Neuhaus: We can speak of God only in the presence of God. It must be admitted, however, that there are many Jews, and many Christians, who are very skeptical about the encounter in which we are engaged. It might be useful for us to talk a little about how we personally, you and I, became involved in the Christian-Jewish dialogue, and why it is a matter of such abiding concern to us. There are Jews who wonder about Klenicki and Christians who wonder about Neuhaus, perhaps thinking that there is something wrong with Jews who are so eager to talk with Christians, and vice versa. Our involvement might be viewed, in a benign way, as a somewhat eccentric interest—or, in a much less benign way, as a suspect conversation in which one or the other or both of us are selling out the interests and beliefs of our communities. I am sorry to say that I have encountered that suspicion among Christians, and I know you are familiar with it from the Jewish side.

Of course, there are very important differences. Jews have always, from their earliest self-awareness, known themselves to be a minority. In the West, they are part of a world that, since the fourth century and still largely today, understands itself to be Christian. Many Christians, on the other hand, were brought up as I was, in a small town and without much awareness of Jews at all. When I was a child, Jews were the Jews of the Old Testament, and not so incidentally, they were also the people who had opposed and killed Jesus. So Jews were either an exotic historical item from ancient days or, to the extent that there were still Jews around, a residual and somewhat puzzling phenomenon. I don't think one would run into this nearly as much today, and it was probably not the experience of many Christians in the early 1940s, but I was certainly taught in cate-chism class that it was a simple matter of fact that Jews have suffered so much in history because, at the cruci-fixion of Jesus, they had cried, "Let his blood be upon us and upon our children." Thus they had invoked the blood curse upon themselves.

The idea of the blood curse has been so thoroughly criticized in our day that it sounds like an anachronis-tic horror. And of course the teaching *was* horrible, and we are now dreadfully aware of the historical ramifica-tions of it, but the odd thing is that, when I was a twelve- or thirteen-year-old child, it didn't make much of an im-pression on me. As best I can recall, I assumed that the teaching made sense, but it did not seem very impor-tant. It was not until college that I met Judaism in the person of Jews.

In any event, at Concordia Theological Seminary in the late 1950s I was much impressed by Rabbi Sol Ber-nards. As you know, he was one of your predecessors in interreligious affairs at the Anti-Defamation League, and a pioneer in the current phase of the Christian-Jewish dialogue. He visited the seminary on a number of occa-sions and I, together with a number of other seminarians, established a warm friendship with him. It was with Sol Bernards's family, for instance, that I first participated in the Passover. But undoubtedly the greatest influence on me was that of the late Rabbi Abraham Joshua Heschel. We came to know one another through our concern about civil rights and the Vietnam war, when I was pastor of a black parish in Brooklyn. In fact, Heschel and I, together with Father Daniel Berrigan, were the first chairmen of what became Clergy Concerned About Vietnam. I have to say, however, that most of the many hundreds of hours we spent together were devoted to discussing not politics and social ethics, but theology. It was largely through Heschel that I was forced to recognize the importance of pondering the mystery of Living Judaism, the continuation of Judaism after Christ, along the lines explored by Saint Paul in Romans 9 through 11. In continuing conversations with Jews such as you and Rabbi David Novak, it has become ever more clear to me that, far from being an optional concern of a few Christians who are interested in that sort of thing, the question of the relationship between Judaism and Christianity holds momentous import for a proper biblical understanding of the Christian reality itself.

More than Toleration

Klenicki: Richard, it's a very good idea to use biographical sketches in our discussion. Lately, there has been a trend in theological research, as you well know, stressing the importance of the autobiographic element in the experience of God.

I was born and educated in Argentina, but I finished my philosophical studies and was ordained a rabbi in Cincinnati, Ohio. Argentina is 90 percent Catholic. That doesn't mean that most people act as Catholics; quite the contrary—most are Catholics only in name. Living in Argentina shaped my life, especially my spiritual life. My parents are originally from Poland. They came to Argentina before the Second World War. There are great similarities between prewar Poland and Argentina. Both of them are predominantly Catholic countries, and they have similar social stratifications. There is the presence of the army and the aristocracy, the working class, and then those who are not in any of those categories—like Protestants and Jews, who always played a secondary role in the life of both countries. Also, by constitutional law, the president and vice president have to be Catholics and the official religion of the country is Roman Catholicism.

So as a Jew, you feel from birth that you are a stranger in your own country, even though there is toleration of Jews in Argentina. I dislike the word "toleration" thoroughly, for it makes you feel that you are a second-class citizen.

Neuhaus: I hope we will come back to the difference between toleration and genuine pluralism.

Klenicki: Yes, we should. When I was young I was sent to public school in the morning, and to Hebrew school in the afternoon. I do not know if we lived an "Argentinian" way of life, if there is such a thing. As Jews, we lived the inward life of a minority, following the spirit of Eastern Europe. Mine was a neo-traditional home in the "pampas."

And that was my reality until I went into high school. My high school was like a typical French *liceea.*

8

Neuhaus: It was not a Jewish school?

Klenicki: No. At that time there were only public schools. Later on, the Jewish community developed a sort of parochial education, if I may call it that. My high school opened up a new perspective for me, not the world of Shalom Aleichim that I read about in Yiddish, but a new world. We studied foreign languages: English, and French, German, Italian, and classical tradition—Latin. And then I woke up to Western literature and started having contacts with some of my friends in high school who were Catholics. The high school was divided into two ideological fronts: there was the neo-Marxist front and the so-called reactionary right-wing religious students. I was critical of the Marxist group.

Neuhaus: What years are we talking about?

Klenicki: Well, I'm talking about the early fifties in Argentina. This was under the dictatorship of General Perón. I started reading Catholic literature. I discovered François Mauriac. Through Mauriac I discovered a Jewish writer, Elie Wiesel, whose first book had an introduction by that French writer.

After high school I got involved with Catholic groups who were studying philosophy. There were practically no good professors at the school of philosophy. Any teachers of importance were expelled by the Perónist government, and replaced with second-rate teachers. There was a whole underground system of study groups in churches and community centers trying to fill the gap in the scholarly situation in the country. I got acquainted at that time with a philosopher who was very influential in the democratization of the Catholic community in Argentina—Jacques Maritain. Maritain was a great influence on me, together with Martin Buber and

9

Franz Rosenzweig, whom I "discovered" through German Jewish friends.

Neuhaus: And so, ironically, Roman Catholic thinkers such as Mauriac and Maritain played an important part in your appreciation of Jewish thought?

Klenicki: Exactly. I appreciated Catholic thought but remained a committed Jew. Some friends of mine who had very poor Jewish backgrounds converted to Catholicism. That was not my case, and never would have been, because I was thoroughly convinced of my Judaism and thoroughly committed to it. But I was also trying to understand others as people of God. From Argentina I went to Cincinnati to study at the Hebrew Union College. There I had that very special experience of America which was for me a discovery—pluralism. I remember that I saw a sign on a wall saying, "Let us pray together for peace," signed by the bishop of Cincinnati, a rabbi, and a pastor. I couldn't believe my eyes. I wrote about this to my father. I was so excited about it! And I was touched by their announcement. I wanted to share that feeling with my father. His response was very simple: "Be careful. They might convert you." He was reacting from another world, and I was experiencing the pluralistic reality of a new society.

Lifting Up Differences

Neuhaus: We can come back to autobiographical factors that have shaped our perceptions, but it might be worth-

while to say something more about the difference between toleration and pluralism. Toleration is a matter of
allowing or permitting the existence of other religions
and viewpoints. As you say, there was toleration in
Argentina, and of course there had been a long European
tradition of toleration. In the United States, on the other
hand, one discovers pluralism. You noted earlier the way
"dialogue" has become a word tattered and wearied by
overuse, and the same is true of "pluralism." And yet
they are both—or they both should be—vibrant words.
Let me suggest that one difference between toleration
and pluralism is that pluralism requires real engagement with one another in a shared community.

Klenicki: On equal terms.

Neuhaus: Yes, on equal terms, although that does not
mean that there are not deep differences between the
two traditions, nor should it suggest indifference to conflicting truth claims. But it does mean that each recognizes the other and respects the other as a participant
in a community. I do not mean the historical community that is America, although the American context con-
tributes powerfully to the possibility of the kind of conversation we have. I mean rather the community of faith
in the God of Abraham, Isaac, Jacob, and Jesus, ac-
knowledging that that faith is understood differently by
each of us. But this is precisely the meaning of pluralism: it is not only the acknowledgment of differences,
but also the engagement of differences. In our dialogue
we need to lift up differences more, and do so without
fear that it is going to jeopardize feelings of cordiality or
good will. Paradoxically, we discover our unity much
more fully and more deeply when we work through our
differences. So much of what is called dialogue in the
American situation is really the practice of indifference.

We say we are "engaged in dialogue" when too often we seem to mean that we've agreed to pretend either that there are no really important differences between us or that any differences we do recognize don't matter much. But neither of those pretensions is true in the relationship between Jews and Christians. And so also with respect to pluralism. The statement that ours is a pluralistic society often seems to indicate what I have called the monism of indifference. In other words, we pretend that our differences make no difference. Genuine pluralism recognizes not only that the exploration of differences is much more interesting intellectually and spiritually, but also that it is the only path to authentic unity. Superficiality in the dialogue can only feed the suspicions of those who view it with skepticism or even hostility.

Klenicki: You are right in using the word "difference." It's not only the difference between us, but also the exercise of this difference. Pluralism allows for a free exercise of our commitments, and in the dialogue experience, I talk to you as a Jewish person, and you respond as a Christian person.

Neuhaus: Emphatically.

Klenicki: The interfaith dialogue entails the active presence of people with equal rights. It also entails a difference. I'm not superior to you, or vice versa. We follow different ways to God, and this will be true until that time, the prophetic days, when we will all recognize the one God, our Redeemer. But until then, we have to understand each other and to share our spiritualities. Sharing does not mean syncretism. It is simply partaking of God's presence and our personal experience. Very traditionalist groups in my community fear this aspect of dialogue. Orthodoxy in particular feels that to share is to lose identity and become assimilated. But the reality is quite different. It is possible to share only when one is totally committed to God, living out one's relationship to God in daily life.

Neuhaus: It should also be admitted that the problems people have with pluralism also extend to ecumenism among Christians. Whether we're talking about the World Council of Churches or the dialogue between Lutherans and Roman Catholics, ecumenism must never mean surrendering confessional integrity for the sake of an appearance of agreement. So also is this emphatically the case in Jewish-Christian encounter. The only Jew that it is rewarding to be in dialogue with is a Jew who is emphatically Jewish. And, of course, the obverse is equally the case. Otherwise we are only playing a game of "let's pretend."

Klenicki: Real dialogue is more than human relations. It is an encounter of hearts, like ours, a friendship in God. This special interpersonal relationship, a process of years, now faces a challenge: how to implement it at the pew level. Our challenge is to project our dialogue of faith to churches and synagogues, that is, to go beyond academic encounters. To meet is, as I said before, to share and to understand. It is only by sharing that I can be spiritually in the place of the other, having a feeling of the Christian experience of God, penetrating into the mystery of religious awe. This was my own experience at the seminary when I wrote my philosophy thesis on Saint John of the Cross and mysticism. Saint John of the Cross was, as you know, a sixteenth-century Spanish mystic and poet. I read him in high school as part of my studies of Spanish literature, and his spirituality was of great interest for my generation.

Neuhaus: You have that in common with Pope John Paul II. John Paul II has also made a particular study of Saint John of the Cross.

Klenicki: I know. At a recent meeting with the pope I mentioned the subject of my thesis. He was touched by that, smiled, embraced me, and said, "Welcome. We are now colleagues in Saint John of the Cross."

The two of us, like many readers of the Spanish mystics, share Saint John's poetry and spiritual perceptions, but differ in the final consideration of his message. This is exemplified in the difference between the pope's approach to the text and my own. John Paul II analyzed the mystics' relationship to and treatment of Catholic tradition. My thesis was a study of the technical mystical language of Saint John. I read him out of my religious tradition and a Jewish mystical interest in order to "sense" his "numinous" feeling for God in the mystical experience, and its closeness to cabalistic appreciation. Since my youth, I have felt close to Saint John of the Cross's concept of the "dark night of the soul" and the human search for God's reality. There was one point where I could not follow Saint John, while the future pope could: that is, the acceptance of Jesus as the light for the dark night of the soul. Jesus was not part of my experience. I could understand the poet's living encounter with him as part of his spirituality, but Jesus was foreign to mine. I could sense a mystical progress toward union with God, but the end result, Jesus as Savior, was totally out of my own feeling and acceptance.

Dialogue as Call from God

Neuhaus: Exactly. We will have to come back to the question of Jewish perceptions of Jesus, but with what you have just said our conversation takes an unexpected but happy turn. I do not know how much weight to attach to John Paul's statement to you, but it certainly is the case that we encounter one another as believers today in the dark night of the soul, to use the phrase of Saint John of the Cross. That is, dialogue is a work of God which we do not pretend to understand. It is not simply something that *we* decide to do, for whatever reason. Surely, we have decided that it is important for Christians and Jews to be in dialogue, but there is a prior decision, a decision by God. This, it seems to me, is the underlying intuition—that God is not yet finished with us Christians and Jews. As Saint Paul repeatedly says, it is not yet clear what we are to become; we see through a glass darkly. The reality that we call Christianity or Judaism has not yet assumed its definitive form. History is open, and we are both defined by our openness to the future and to one another.

As a Christian, I believe that the self-revelation of God occurred in Jesus Christ, in his death, his resurrection, and the promise of his coming again. But it is precisely this promise that reminds us that we are still a people "on the way," that the final configuration of the promised fulfillment is still in the future. Nowhere do we find that more forcefully and compellingly expressed than in Paul's writing to the Romans, especially when he dwells on the mysterious connection between Israel and the church. We do not understand exactly what it is that God is doing in this dialogue between Christians and Jews, but I believe it is his work before it is ours.

15

We Lutherans speak frequently of the *deus absconditus,* the hiddenness of God and his ways, and that applies also to this dialogue.

And all of this, of course, underscores what you earlier said about faith, that here too we must follow his leading even when we do not know where he is leading. Surely there have been very major changes, and we, Christians and Jews, have been changed by the new perceptions of each other. Our particular dialogue is dated from the last several decades, but we must also remember earlier Jewish-Christian encounters. One thinks of such major Jewish figures as Franz Rosenzweig, Martin Buber, and Leo Baeck in this century. They were truly pioneers, and anyone who doubts that their contribution to the history of dialogue in this century has made a real difference is, I am afraid, simply ill-informed. But finally I do believe that the dialogue is more than a history of encounters that we can document. It is, as we Christians would say, a movement of the Holy Spirit leading us into the fuller truth about ourselves and about our relationship to our "elder brothers" in the covenant. It is, in short, a walk of faith.

Klenicki: I am delighted that you pointed that out. I like to call the present state of the dialogue a call of God. I feel that at this point in history, after centuries of Christian triumphalism, our own history of exile and return, the death of Auschwitz, and the return to the Promised Land through the creation of the state of Israel, we are called to an encounter of soul and heart. It is a time of *crisis* (following the Greek meaning of the word), a time of decision: a time of looking for new roads to witness God. We Jews have to express the covenantal relationship beyond our illusions of a century of emancipation in Europe—illusions that ended in the gas chambers. We have to realize also that we are not alone, we are with

16

others, and God is calling us to joint witness, though all of us, Jews and Christians, are committed to our own particular method of covenantal testimony.

It is not easy to accept such a goal, to understand our vocations of peace. Christians and Jews are together in the denial of this vocation, though for different reasons, in spite of the fact that we might at times express our conviction of being together before God. For Jews, memories of the past, our experience of "Christian charity" for Judaism and the Jewish people through the centuries and up to our own days, as well as Christian triumphalism—the Christian denial of Jews in God's design—are realities difficult to overcome. They come back again and again in words and gestures. I am concerned about a Jewish triumphalism arising from memories and pain.

Christians are not free of a similar triumphalism. There are those who stress Christianity as the culmination of God's covenant with Abraham and who deny Judaism as a religious commitment fulfilled by its own history. Such views mark a step backward in the dialogue and recall medieval triumphalists.

In 1987, Eugene J. Fisher, who is in charge of Catholic-Jewish relations at the National Conference of Catholic Bishops, and I published a collection of the writings of John Paul II, and his vision of Judaism is quite different.

Neuhaus: Including all of the pope's speeches?

Klenicki: Yes, up to July 1987. The pope emphasizes in his writings the eternity of the God-Israel covenant and the ongoing meaningful mission of Judaism, and he condemns anti-Semitism as a sin. His words express an acceptance of Judaism and the Jewish people as "the other," using Buberian terminology. By stressing this concept, John Paul asks Christians to overcome centuries of teaching of contempt. Simultaneously, however, John Paul II continues to use terms of contempt in some of his Sunday homilies in his St. Peter's public meetings. The New Testament, a sacred text, still requires expounding of its meaning after two thousand years, especially in regard to Jews and the Judaism contemporary to Jesus. The text alone, without any explanation, sounds anti-Semitic in some places, even though the text itself may have been written by a Jew who was critical of his fellow Jews for not accepting Jesus as the Messiah, the Christ. This is not explained in John Paul's homilies, and the pope's reading of the New Testament often appears critical and anti-Semitic. It seems as if it is difficult in many Christian circles to accept Judaism.

There is an ambiguity for Christians in accepting Judaism as a still creative force, a meaningful covenant with God, because they still have a certain triumphalism that denies Judaism in God's design.

Neuhaus: Yes, two thousand years later we must recognize with a new lucidity that the New Testament refers us back again to this question of engaging Living Judaism, not simply the Judaism that is seen as a residual and somewhat embarrassing phenomenon left over from the Old Testament.

Klenicki: Or as merely the preparation for the coming of Christianity.

Walking "The Way"

Neuhaus: Certainly this has been the Christian problem. We have too often thought that Jews once had a place in salvation history but that they lost that place after the coming of Christ. I am afraid this is still the dominant view in large sectors of Christianity. Here in America in the last decade we've seen an upsurge of fundamentalist and dispensationalist religion. It has a great deal to say about Jews and about Israel as they relate to "Bible prophecy" about the end time. This is an intriguing development in American culture and religion, and one that I think has to be explored sympathetically. But it also has great weaknesses. Jews in that scheme of things are given an important place in the apocalyptic working out of the end time, but Jews have no role or only a negative role in terms of the salvation secured through Christ. Jews remain as much of a theological embarrassment, so to speak, as they were to Christianity in the Middle Ages. Obviously, the practical support that these premillennialist dispensationalists give to Israel can be welcomed, but at the same time we must note that it is an approach that does not begin to penetrate the questions posed by Saint Paul in, for example, Romans 9 through 11.

Klenicki: I think, Richard, that it is very important for us to pose and ponder the meaning of the so-called first century. That is, let's examine the first century, not with a sense of confrontation as was common in the Middle Ages, but by going back to the roots that are common to Jews and Christians. I now use the term "the first century" without any inner problems, but years ago I wouldn't have used that term, because I thought the first century was "a Christian invention" . . .

Neuhaus: A bit of Christian triumphalism.

Klenicki: Yes. Now I realize that it was also a "first century" for us Jews. The destruction of the Second Temple in the year 70 marked the beginning of a new period of spirituality that lasted until the twentieth century, breaking down through the hell of Auschwitz. So I think that the first century C.E. was a beginning for both Christians and Jews. The first century forms the roots of the tree that grew into different branches, if I may use an image of St. Paul. Christianity is a branch of the biblical tradition, just as is the Judaism that branched out through the rabbinical interpretation of the Bible.

Neuhaus: Your mention of the first century raises another consideration. While it is critically important for the Christian-Jewish dialogue to engage differences, it is also necessary to clear away so-called differences that get in the way of understanding. Many Christians have accepted antitheses between Judaism and Christianity that are simply not justified. For instance, I was taught both as a child and all the way through seminary that one difference between Judaism and Christianity, between the Old Testament and the New, is that Judaism and the Old Testament are totally preoccupied with the law, whereas with Christianity came the dawning of the grace of God. The law has to do only with the demands that God places upon us, whereas Christianity brought the good news of the mercy of God. Here again Heschel was very important to my thinking back in the sixties. He instructed me in a truth that Christians should not have forgotten, namely, in the ways in which the law in the Hebrew Scriptures is also, so to speak, gospel. One thinks of the psalms—say, Psalm 119, with its exultation in the law precisely as the evidence of God's mercy. Obviously, talk about the grace and mercy of God engages very significant differences between Christians and Jews, but it seems to me terribly important that Christians see how Jews exult in the grace that is expressed in a way of life, or *Halakah*, that is premised entirely upon the gratuitous love of God in the election of Israel.

Klenicki: You just mentioned a key word, Richard, the word *Halakah.* That word immediately brings to my mind the Italian saying "Traduttore, traditori," which means "He who translates commits treason." And that's what happened in the relationship between Jews and Christians. Unfortunately, Christians do not think in Hebrew, and we, unfortunately, do not think in Greek. In any translation, the translator's own ideas are projected in his or her choice of words. A good example of this is the term *Halakah,* which has been translated as "nomos," or "law." But Halakah is not law. *Halakah* comes from the verb *halah,* which means "to go"; it is a way of being and acting. The rabbis used this term to convey the idea that to be religious is a way of being; thus Halakah is concerned with the observance of the Sabbath, daily prayers, the keeping of kashrut, not mixing milk with meat, and many of the other daily details of leading a religious life. The word *Halakah* was not foreign to early Christianity, and Jesus was a follower of Halakah himself. So when Jesus said, "I am the way," what was he saying, exactly? What word did he have in mind? I feel that he had the word *Halakah* in mind—meaning that he was the way for the world.

Neuhaus: That is very suggestive for our Christian understanding of what our Lord meant when he said, "I am the way, the truth, and the life." And of course this touches on the subject that we can never get very far away from, and should not want to get away from. The subject, of course, is the figure of Jesus himself. A rabbi friend with great theological acumen used to say to me, "Ah, Richard, if you could only drop the Christology—if you could only drop this obsessive concentration on Jesus, then there would be removed a great obstacle between us." But I think that he was wrong because, for us Christians, Jesus is also the way, the entry point, into our relationship with Judaism.

Klenicki: Your relationship with God, not necessarily with Judaism.

Neuhaus: Yes, our relationship with God, ultimately and most importantly, but also with Judaism. And I do not think the two can be easily separated. To encounter Jesus is to encounter Judaism. It is because of Jesus that the encounter with Judaism is not optional for Christians. Judaism would not be so important for Christians were it not for Jesus the Jew. This is the crucial question that people like Rosenzweig pondered so creatively, and it must command our attention as well. What are the ramifications of the Christian belief that history is centered in Jesus whom we call the Christ? What does it mean that, as Saint Paul says, God has not broken his covenantal promise with Israel? Do we Christians worship a God other than the God whom Jesus called Father, who is of course also the God of Abraham, Isaac, and Jacob? And then this further question cannot be evaded: Do we worship a God other than the God whom you worship as a Jew? In reflecting on all of these questions, it seems to me that Jesus is the inescapable nexus.

Jesus and the Mission of the Jews

Klenicki: This is a very touchy subject. In general, the very word "Jesus" whips up very negative feelings in Jews. It's mixed with our history, with our direct memories, or with the memories transmitted to us through our parents. It's a constant reality. I use the word "Jesus" with no problem at all, but I know my father would have problems using it. I would feel uneasy saying "Jesus Christ," because I cannot agree with the Messianic vocation of Jesus. I think that in the dialogue, once we overcome prejudice, we Jews have to overcome the weight of memories—the castrating effect of memories on us, because by mentioning Jesus, we remember two thousand years of persecution—and we sense that persecution even today in the left-wing and right-wing attacks on Judaism and the state of Israel.

We have to understand Jesus as part of God's design. I'm so careful when I say that because I immediately feel that somebody will jump up and say, "Well, now, you are on the way to conversion," which is not true. In trying to understand Jesus as part of God's design I have been very much influenced by another reading of my youth, the writings of Elijah Benamozeg, an Italian rabbi and theologian who died in the 1900s. Benamozeg wrote on Christianity, examining the religious and theological meaning of Christianity. He pointed out that there is a close relationship between Noah and Jesus. Noah is the first covenant of God. We in Judaism don't consider the relationship between God and Adam and Eve as a covenant. That was only a relationship. The relationship between God and Noah, on the other hand, was the first covenant entailing a set of commands, the Noachic laws of moral, individual, and community behavior. According to Benamozeg, that first covenant between God and humanity through Noah didn't work out because Noah didn't really fulfill God's command of bringing the whole of humanity to God through a moral commitment. Jesus appears to continue the task given to Noah. Jesus is God's instrument to bring humanity to the eternal. Jesus is seen not as the Messianic fulfillment but as a road to God, a way for humanity to reach God. I do not accept the Messianic dimension of Jesus, but I do accept Jesus.

Neuhaus: There is much in what you say that we as Christians should embrace. Some might dispute the numbering of the covenants, saying that the covenant was first with the creation and was renewed with Noah. But certainly there is the covenant that entails the election of Abraham and all that is involved in Genesis 12, as you point out. Maybe we should come back to the ways in which that election of Israel is not simply for Israel, but is for all of humanity, for all the nations.

Klenicki: To become a light to the nations.

Neuhaus: Indeed, to become a light to the nations. And, of course, we Christians see that promise fulfilled in Jesus, whom we call the light of the world, a favorite metaphor in John's gospel. This matter of Israel's mission to the nations is especially stressed by Isaiah, and it is puzzling to many Christians that so many Jews are nervous about this idea of the mission of Israel. It is precisely that election and mission of Israel that makes it possible to understand Jesus and his role in the salvific purpose of God to extend the Abrahamic covenant to the whole of humanity through the church. Of course, we touch upon some painfully controverted issues here— the way in which Jesus is the fulfillment of Judaism, or

24

an extension of Judaism, or the exercise of the mission of Judaism. From the Christian side, it all too often happens that we embrace an idea of supersession in which the "fulfillment" in Jesus entirely eclipses and makes obsolete the reality of Judaism. We isolate Jesus the Christ from the very history of salvation that gives substance to our saying that Jesus is the Christ. It is so very important for Christians to see that the recognition of Jesus as the Christ was a Jewish recognition and was articulated in Jewish terms. The particularity of Jesus as a Jew is not an incidental particularity.

At a very abstract level one can speculate about whether God could have revealed himself, could have become incarnate (a very easily misunderstood expression for Christians and Jews alike!), in some other history. Maybe the Christ could have been a Roman or a Persian or a Greek. But to say that he is the Christ is to say that he is the anointed one and, were he a Roman, of what sacred story would he have been the anointed seal? Of what history of promise would he have been the fulfillment? No, it is of *this* history, *this* people, *this* promise that he is the Christ. Here is an odd thing: Christians who break Jesus away from the Jewish reality think that they are elevating Christ and the church when in fact they are eliminating the very foundation that gives meaning to our affirmation of Christ and the church. Saying that the church is the "New Israel" only makes sense with reference to Israel. Here is a paradox that I suppose every community tends to forget. If you so elevate the distinctive claims of your own community as to exclude what is valid in the claims of other communities, you in fact end up diminishing the significance of your own community, reducing its claims to a kind of sectarian self-aggrandizement and boasting.

Klenicki: Saint Augustine, who was not a friend of my

people, has in one of his books a phrase that I had to study in Latin when I was in high school. He says, "Let us have mercy upon words." Words have really hurt us. Christians had no mercy with our Hebrew words. I would blame the Christian community for diminishing the meaning of sacred words because of its use and abuse of certain terms. Sometimes we Jews decide not to use words like "mission," "covenant," or "election," because they sound too Christian, even though they are a part of our own heritage. And you just used a word that makes me feel uneasy: the word "fulfillment," because of its triumphalistic overtones. We can apply this noun to the rabbinic expounding of the biblical text in the first century, the fulfillment in history of the Sinai God/Israel relationship. That was done through the Mishnah, which is the Halakic interpretation of the Bible, the interpretation of God's command in everyday religious life. There was also a literary explanation of the text called the Midrash, which was known to Jesus, as can be seen in New Testament texts. We feel that we have been fulfilled through these interpretations. But that fulfillment—as I said earlier—breaks down in our time. Now we have to search for a new fulfillment of our relationship with God after the exile of the Holocaust.

The Question of Conversion

Neuhaus: I suppose here we must address the question of Jewish fulfillment through conversion to Christ. Do you agree?

Klenicki: Yes I think so. I think that is very, very important.

Neuhaus: The uneasiness you express with regard to the word "fulfillment" becomes very painful at this point. As you are well aware, those who engage in "the mission to the Jews" insist that in no sense does a Jew stop being a Jew when he becomes a Christian. On the contrary, the claim is that he or she then becomes most fully Jewish. This issue came up again in the recent controversy over Edith Stein, a Jew who converted to Christianity and who has now been beatified by the Roman Catholic Church. It is also of more than passing interest to note how many of the major Christian figures in the Jewish-Christian dialogue of this century have been Jewish converts to Christianity. Indeed, those in the leadership of "the mission to the Jews" have also, more often than not, been Jews who professed to find the fulfillment of their Judaism in Christ. Obviously, this reality raises hard questions about everything we have been saying with respect to the continuing role of Living Judaism in God's saving purposes.

Klenicki: Now, I wonder what term you would use if you were converting a pagan to Christianity? Would you say that that person had fulfilled his or her religious desire for God?

Neuhaus: It's an important question, and I expect that it should be answered in the affirmative. In recent times Karl Rahner has perhaps been the most thorough in arguing that in Christ there is the fulfillment of humanity, of the *humanum.* Nothing that is authentically human is alien to God in Christ; by entering life in Christ, one is entering into the fullest expression of all that is authentically human. Here we come upon

Rahner's much-discussed and, I think, frequently mis-understood idea of the "anonymous Christian," an idea that can easily be distorted into another form of tri-umphalism. It can be taken to mean that everyone is really a Christian but that, for whatever reason, many people do not know that they are Christians. In that ver-sion of "anonymous Christian," people—including Jews—are not given space to be the religious individu-als they believe and declare themselves to be. That said, however, I do not see how an orthodox Christian can deny that, in truth, Jesus the Christ is "the beginning and the end," the one from whom all comes and to whom all tend.

But it would be a grave mistake to lose sight of the singularity of the relationship between Christian and Jew. Here again we are returned to the particularity fac-tor. I do not know if the old doggerel "How odd of God / To choose the Jews" was intended in an anti-Semitic way or not (though I think not), but it contains a pro-found truth. That is, if one begins with an abstract uni-versalistic idea of a divinity setting about the redemp-tion of his creation, he did it in a very odd way. With all the other candidates available, there seems to be no good reason why he should have elected the tribe of Abraham—or, for that matter, why he shouldn't have made his decisive move a few thousand years earlier, or later. Viewed by human reason, God's particularity can-not help but seem arbitrary. And, of course, in the Chris-tian telling of the story this oddness continues with Jesus, the disciples, and the founding of the church. The story is ludicrously audacious if it is not true. The disciples were hardly what we would think of as mate-rial for canonization, and many take it as evidence of the truth of the story that that fact is made so embar-rassingly clear by the disciples themselves, who tell the story in the New Testament. To be sure, the scandal that

28

trumps all others is that the redemption of the world is effected by the shameful execution of a doubtfully credentialled rabbi on a dung hill outside the walls of a minor provincial capital.

The point I want to underscore again is this matter of particularity. In response to the question of whether or not the pagan or *humanum* is fulfilled in Christ, the answer must be yes. But there is something most particular, most singular, about the relationship between Christians and Jews. For Christians, talking with Jews is not the same as talking with pagans or Muslims or Buddhists or "humanity in general." In conversation with Judaism, we are in conversation with our own story of salvation. This does not make the conversation any easier. In fact, in some ways it makes it harder, for both Christian and Jew. The Jew cannot help but wonder whether the true aim of the Christian, after all is said and done, is the conversion of the Jew. And the Christian, it seems to me, is not permitted to deny—after affirming with Saint Paul that the covenant with Israel is irrevocable—that Jesus is the fulfillment of the covenant. For all kinds of powerfully human reasons the Christian in dialogue may be tempted to deny that. But I believe that the Jewish partner in dialogue must want the Christian to resist any temptation that would make him less authentically Christian.

At the same time, both Christian and Jew must be pledged to exploring the ways in which their authentic beliefs may not be in conflict but can actually be a bond of unity in common faith. One such belief, certainly, is a common understanding of history as being open to an eschatological promise not yet consummated. Our disagreements cannot be the final word because God has not yet spoken the final word. Or, if some Christian would object that the final word has been spoken in Jesus, I would amend that to say that the final form of that word has not yet been spoken in the promised Messianic Age. Therefore, with both Christian and Jew, there should be a faith-based humility, and the awareness that such humility is not a matter of compromise but a matter of fidelity to the truth that God's future is beyond our understanding and control. Neither of us can "get it all together" until God has gotten it all together in the coming of his kingdom. In this way, our disagreements, along with the yearning of the whole creation (Romans 8), must be marked by a powerful element of provisionality.

I recall Heschel asking me at the lighting of the Sabbath candles in his home, "Would you, as a Christian, really want a world in which these candles were no longer lit and these Jewish prayers were no longer said?" The answer must be an unqualified no. Of course, the proponents of the mission to the Jews would agree with that in their own way, contending that Jewish Christians would continue to light the candles and say the prayers, and would be giving up nothing of their Jewishness—except for their former rejections of Jesus as Messiah. Such an answer, I am afraid, is often given in too facile a manner. We Christians must try harder to understand the Jews who are also seeking to work out their salvation in fear and trembling and to follow the leading of God, and we must also try to understand why such Jews view conversion as a horror, as a betrayal of their divine vocation.

Klenicki: One of our great thinkers, Franz Rosenzweig, wrote—after the First World War, after his own experience of going back to Judaism instead of converting to Christianity—that there is a difference between Jews and Christians in relating to God. We Jews have been with the Father from the very beginning, from Genesis 12 where God chooses and calls Abraham to be a community with a purpose, while Christians need Jesus to reach the Father. While this does make a difference, it also allows for a deeper dialogue among Jews and Christians. We are unified by the fact that we have the Father in common, making us brothers. Perhaps Jews are the older brothers, but we are brothers in dialogue. I feel that perhaps something else that is divisive between Jews and Christians is the word "salvation," which you have used several times. I would use, instead, the word "redemption." My relationship with God is not a relationship by which I will be "saved." As a partner of God in the covenant, it is my obligation to make every effort in redeeming the world, in making the kingdom of God a reality, achieving the kingdom of goodness in this universe and in this time of our being in history. So perhaps, in the dialogue, in the relationship that we have, we have to examine the question: What is redemption? What is salvation? How can we work together within our respective commitments for the kingdom of God?

Regarding Heaven and Earth

Neuhaus: It is true, I earlier used the terms "salvation" and "redemption" more or less interchangeably. To be sure, many Christians use "salvation" in a quite different way, meaning their own individual "being saved," their own—to put it bluntly—ticket to heaven. That can be a legitimate way of speaking but it also tends to lose the quality of the redemption you are speaking of, the cosmic fulfillment for which the whole creation yearns. And that is beyond doubt a very Christian way of speaking as well, which is obvious in the majestic cosmic hymns of Romans 8 and Philippians 2, for example. And so, just as in Gene-

31

sis 12 the covenant with Israel extends to the whole of humanity in which Israel is to be this redemptive agent, so also in Jesus, it can be said, a very large part of this humanity beyond Judaism is incorporated into the covenant. All who are now in that one covenant with the Father are the agents of Genesis 12 updated, so to speak, for the redemption of the entire world.

But here let me put a question to you, Leon, about something that confuses many Christians. You speak about the redemption of the world, and I expected you would also say that it is God who is redeeming the world, but that we are called to partnership with God in this task. You also used the expression "establishing the kingdom of God." Many Christians say that one critical difference between Jews and Christians is that your understanding of redemption, or salvation, or the kingdom of God, is entirely this-worldly. Christians, on the other hand, look to another world of which this world is already part, and, of course, to the resurrection of the dead.

Klenicki: We Jews have a great concern for the world in which we live. We feel that it is part of creation and was given to us by God as a gift and as an obligation. In the creation, for example, Adam and Eve are given specific tasks and also a prohibition—not to eat of the tree of knowledge. Their action in doing so is a transgression of God's friendship. We do not consider it a sin. The rabbis and our sages did not consider it a sin, but rather a failure in fulfilling the creative friendship between God and the first couple, Adam and Eve. Creation is central to our thought, and we express it hopefully in our daily prayers. We glorify creation and praise God for its renewal every day.

Neuhaus: Do you see that as different from your understanding of the Christian view of the creation?

Klenicki: We share the belief in God's creation, but Jews in the perspective of both time and eternity continue to think in terms of their duties in this world. We do think in terms of the other world, referring to it with the biblical term "sheol," which later on came to mean hell. But in the very beginning, especially in the text of the book of Samuel, it meant a place where souls are in suspension, in a kind of eternal peace. It was only later, much later, especially during the rabbinic period and then in the Middle Ages, that we emphasized the concept of another world as reward or punishment. During the Middle Ages, times of persecution and suffering, the concept of the other world became a hopeful oasis of peace. I feel, however, that there is danger in emphasizing the concept of this world, for we might become so much a part of this world that we become indifferent to the task given by God. That task is the sanctification of everyday life in order to implement the covenant.

Neuhaus: Do you, as a Jew today, Leon, think about your eternal destiny as a member of the covenant community? Is the idea of an eternal destiny—heaven, hell, judgment, perfect communion with the absolute, with God—is that a key part of your own piety, your own spirituality?

Klenicki: Yes, it is, but in the sense of my personal obligation of making this world a better world, of bringing the kingdom of God, which is the prelude to the coming of the Messiah. I think of death without any fear. I think of death as a sort of eternal rest, a time of peace before the coming of the Messiah. I cannot imagine a hell and a paradise. For me, hell and paradise are here on earth. Auschwitz was a good representation of hell. The indifference of humanity to human suffering—that's another form of hell. But after death, I know God will ask me a question in the best tradition of Hasidic theological understanding. God will ask me if I, Leon Klenicki, a person created by the Eternal to fulfill the covenant of relationship with God, have done enough to improve the human situation.

Neuhaus: And will it, in your understanding, make a difference whether the answer to that question is "yes" or "no"?

Klenicki: Yes, it will make a great difference.

Neuhaus: For Leon Klenicki? Eternally?

Klenicki: Yes, eternally. And I think that also relates to the rest of my community, though my community might not think in those terms because, once again, they fear it sounds too Christian. They fear that these are Christian questions and not Jewish questions, though they are essentially part of our tradition from biblical times to our own days, through centuries of interpretation.

Neuhaus: A good point, but even if we were to stipulate that they are distinctively Christian questions, isn't it, as we suggested earlier, essential to the integrity of the dialogue that Jews be asking Christians Jewish questions, and Christians be asking Jews Christian questions?

The American Connection

Klenicki: That's very, very important. I would point out that such a dialogue should consider the integrity of the other in faith. It should respect differences in trying to comprehend the spiritual depth projected in their responses. This is an obligation for both Jews and Christians. Otherwise we are open to ambiguity—that is, questions and responses of double meaning, obscure and doubtful. The danger in asking Jewish questions of Christians and the reverse is that feelings or passions may be projected rather than thoughtful and reflective considerations. I realized this in my readings of Saint Paul's Epistle to the Romans. I belong to a group of Christians and Jews who have been meeting regularly to study chapters nine through eleven of that letter. It's difficult both in text and in spirit. I ask him—or, rather, his text—questions coming out of first- and second-century Judaism, and I project, at times, my yearning and ambiguity toward Paul and his use and abuse of biblical sources. My ambiguity parallels Paul's ambiguity toward Israel and its place in God's design. Paul conveys a sense of ambiguity that is reflected in later Christianity. That is, Paul expresses the difficulty Christians have in accepting Judaism as a meaningful voice of God, despite the Jesus event. On our side, we feel that Paul illustrates what happened after Constantine when Christianity became the official religion of the Roman Empire: we became second-class citizens in civil rights and in religious considerations. Christianity became the very image and symbol of our oppression. We have to overcome, as I said before, memories and images of this oppression.

I feel that we can do this together in the United States, a pluralistic society, enjoying the constitutional separation of church and state, in this democratic country.

Neuhaus: Especially in the United States, as you say, and that is very important indeed. I think it is no exaggeration to say that here and now, for the first time in history, there is the opportunity and therefore the obligation for Jews and Christians to engage one another in authentic dialogue. Surely, there have been rare individual Jews and rare Christians who have done that in the past, but it was not the engagement of communities. Here there are substantial numbers of Christians and Jews who can reach out to one another. Because of unspeakable tragedy, that is not the case in Germany or in most of the rest of Europe. And of course it is also not the case in Israel, where there is not the pluralistic context that makes such dialogue possible.

But, again, I am not at all sure that we Christians and Jews are acting on the opportunity and obligation that we have here. You and I are convinced that the bond between Christians and Jews can only be securely established on the basis of faith, of believing today, but in that respect I expect that we are in the minority in our communities. I remember some years ago being part of an interfaith panel in a midwestern city. The chairman of the event got up and held forth on how wonderful it was that sitting here in amity were a Catholic, a Protestant, and a Jew. How is this possible? he rhetorically asked. I was hoping he would say something about our community in the God of Abraham, Isaac, and Jacob. But no. He triumphantly concluded, "It is possible because, despite the fact that one is a Catholic and one is a Protestant and one is a Jew, we recognize that we are all Americans!" That was very sad, but not very surprising. Of course it was a very American meeting, and it would be hard to imagine its happening anywhere else. But the point missed is that, while the expression of the bond between us was very American, the reality of that bond was forged not by American civil religion but by the history of God's redemptive work. If I respect you "despite" the fact that you are a Jew, we have made a substantive advance beyond the "toleration" associated with the French Enlightenment and Europe, in which Jews were emancipated in terms of their civil rights as individuals, so long as they didn't disrupt the arrangement by being too Jewish.

Klenicki: Exactly.

Neuhaus: Most important, they were not to be very Jewish in public. But such toleration, as became tragically evident in Europe, was a foundation of sand for the relationship between Jews and Christians. I mean, to put it quite bluntly, why should Christians, especially when they are in the overwhelming majority, care very much about Jews and Judaism? As anti-Semites are always reminding us, here is this small minority, less than three percent of the population, exercising such inordinate influence in "our" society. As much as anti-Semitism may be contained at the moment in American life, we cannot forget that, on the left and right of the social and political spectrum, there are fever swamps that serve as lovely breeding grounds for such resentments. There is no profound and convincing answer to the question of why we must respect Jews and Judaism unless it is found in a religious, theological, and spiritual understanding of the bond between us. All of America's legal and constitutional guarantees are, as James Madison said, just "parchment barriers" to social hostility unless they are backed up by a morally and religiously convincing answer to this question.

But this brings us to a question that I have often had put to me and that you might now address. Many Christians object that everything we're saying is fine when you're talking about Jews such as Abraham Heschel and Leon Klenicki. "What you say about Romans 9 to 11, and the covenant, and Genesis 12, and Isaiah 55, and so forth, that's all very interesting and may well be true," they assert. But in fact, they go on to observe, most of the Jews in America today are quite indifferent to that understanding of a covenantal faith. They are simply "ethnic Jews" who are thoroughly secularized. Therefore, I am told, the foundation that I and others propose for Jewish-Christian relations is almost entirely irrelevant to what is in fact the American situation.

Secularization

Klenicki: Richard, I think it's important to deal with the question of who are the people of God and what are the vocations of God in our respective communities. It is not easy for Jews, especially for a very traditionally oriented group, to deal with the question of who are the people or peoples of God. A recent event will illustrate Jewish distrust of theological dialogue. John Paul II visited the United States and met with Jewish leadership in Miami. The pope was greeted warmly and a speech was read. The text had been prepared carefully, and I remember that in one of the drafts there was a great emphasis on theological concepts. Some representatives vetoed that language, and as a consequence I would say that the final version sounded very secular—tremendously secular for my taste. The theological sections were vetoed by Orthodox colleagues, so the speech was not given in religious terms. The words projected secular feelings and concepts. This speech contrasted sharply with the one given by the pope. This requires much thought on our side. But we suffer a historical reality: there has been a

Christian mutilation of our theological being, because for centuries we have been afraid of expressing our ideas, for fear that that would lead to controversies, disputations, and persecutions as has happened in the past. But the present reality is different. We are free to talk and think. One aspect that needs to be reflected on is how we understand our vocations of being people or peoples of God.

Neuhaus: Here again you raise a question that puzzles many Christians. Christians perceive two phenomena that are in some ways contradictory. On the one hand, it is perceived not only that many Jews are very secular but also that they often seem determined to secularize a society that is, at least demographically speaking, Christian. Thus it is frequently pointed out there appears to be a disproportionate number of Jews in groups such as the American Civil Liberties Union, Norman Lear's People for the American Way, and similar organizations—all of which are viewed as militantly secular and set on perpetuating what has been called "the naked public square," a public life denuded of all religious reference. On the other hand, it is perceived that the Jews who are really serious about being Jewish, such as the Orthodox, are very suspicious about basing Jewish-Christian relations on theological or spiritual or biblical foundations. They don't want to talk theology at all. So it seems that both secular Jews and religious Jews are opposed to the understanding of the dialogue that we want to advance.

Klenicki: Richard, I think we have to go back to the biblical text itself. Take Genesis 12, the first verses, when God calls Abraham, who in the text is Abram, not yet Abraham. God promised to Abram to make out of him and Sarai a *Goy Gadol,* a term that can be translated as "a great community" or "a great nation," and also "a promised land." Notice the peculiar fact that there is no adjective there meaning "religious." It doesn't say "a great, significant, *religious* community," but "a great *community*." I would even say a community with a manifest destiny, but today that language is not proper or acceptable in our society.

Neuhaus: And sometimes the destiny isn't so manifest, even though it remains the destiny.

Klenicki: Exactly. I agree with that. There is a Jewish understanding of the secular and the sacred which is different from what is understood in medieval Christian theology.

I would say that the word "secular" doesn't have the negative connotation for us that it does in Christian understanding. The concept is clearly stated in the *Havdalah* liturgy that we perform at the end of the Sabbath. The community praises the Sabbath rest that is essentially the inner work of recovering God in prayer and study. But we also praise the rest of the week, the secular time, a time devoted to developing God's work of creation.

The Jewish community is not, in that way, only a community of God-oriented people. It's a people with a destiny permeated by the covenant.

Many Jews don't recognize, accept, or understand the covenant relationship. It is ironic that the struggle for human rights, peculiar to many Jewish organizations, reflects a Jewish religious concern about the destiny and the rights of human beings. Also, we have to remember that because of past experiences of suffering and persecution, especially in Europe, even before Hitler, Jews are more interested in civil rights than in the total exercise of the religious life in "the naked public square," to use the title of your book. But this does not mean that we are shy, or that we don't want to show our commitment. It is related to that past history. For that reason, the present reality of American life shows that there is a greater interest in developing and exercising Jewishness.

When I was in Cincinnati studying at the Hebrew Union College in 1959, I remember the importance attached to the fact that we were Americans just like Mr. Jones across the street, both in the teaching of the seminar and in the general attitude of my fellow rabbinical students: we were American citizens outside in the streets, but Jewish in the synagogue or the home. This idea was reflected in our prayer book and in our usage of impeccable English.

There has been a return to traditional values and rituals in order to recover a sense of Jewish experience of God and community. It is a recovery of *Halakah,* a way of covenantal existence framed by contemporary history. This new development is not a negation of Reform Judaism. It is rather a growing in spiritual depth and tradition, projecting it in daily life and the life of the community. Tradition is seen in the way in which the word itself means—that is, "from hand to hand." Tradition is not an end in itself but a way to make meaningful the contemporary experience of God. This is mirrored in the new edition of the Reform prayer book, *Gates of Prayer,* with its increased incorporation of Hebrew texts, its sense of Jewish destiny, and its need to make the present meaningful in closer relationship with our millennial past.

Leon Klenicki and Richard John Neuhaus

The Naked Public Square

Neuhaus: Before moving on, Leon, I wonder if we might pause here a moment. In connection with the point you just raised, you know that there is a great deal of anxiety and agitation in America today about the inroads that have been made by what is called secular humanism. It seems to me—and this ties in with what you were saying earlier—that the organizational leadership of American Judaism for a very long time bought the proposition that the more secular the society is, the better it would be for Jews. So that this desire to be, in public, as indistinguishable as possible in terms of anything distinctively Jewish has carried over into a more general approach to the role of religion in American life. Now, as you say, today there is within Judaism a resurgence of being unapologetically Jewish, in public as well as in private, so that one no longer tries to maintain a low Jewish profile in the hope that—

Klenicki: We will not be discovered.

Neuhaus: Precisely. On the political level—although that of course is far from being the most important level—this was also evident. Here in New York, for example, for a very long time, until Abraham Beam was elected mayor in the early 1970s, Jewish leaders were said to believe that Jews should keep a fairly low profile, and they certainly should not be elected mayor. The idea was that a high profile would arouse latent anti-Semitism and anxieties about "inordinate" Jewish influence in the city. But here we are now, well into Ed Koch's third term as mayor, and it would seem that a good deal has changed on that score. He certainly makes no secret of his Jewishness. But at a deeper level, are you suggesting that this resurgence of an un-apologetic Jewish presence in public may also lead to a reconsideration of the proposition that the more secular the society is, the better it is for Jews?

Klenicki: We have to continue thinking about that, because one of our fears is that whenever organized religion gets into the political arena, it is very dangerous for the Jewish community, as it was in Europe and is now in Latin America where Catholicism is generally not on good terms with minorities, Jews or Protestants.

The present reconsideration of our religious position—I am thinking mainly in terms of the U.S. experience—relates to two events and a movement of renewal. The two events were the Holocaust and the creation of the state of Israel, two events that mark a "before" and "after" in our history of redemption.

The renewal movement is the Havurah movement, which was known already in the first century C.E. and was known to Jesus and his *Havurah* of apostles. The word means "fellowship," a circle of friends devoted to prayer and study. The Havurah movement today is a response to the challenge of being religious in the twentieth century. It is essentially *Teshuvah*, a word generally translated as "repentance," but it is more than repentance; it is a reckoning of the soul, a reconsideration of what has gone wrong in our life and a response to that reckoning. How do we respond to the crisis that we are facing now? Facing more and more . . .

Neuhaus: Where does one see this Havurah movement in Judaism today?

Klenicki: As I said before, the Havurah movement originally appeared in Jewish life in the first century B.C.E., prior to the coming of our era, and developed into two kinds of fellowship. The first is represented by the communities founded by the Essenes, especially the monastery founded at Qumran, near the Dead Sea. We know about them from the Dead Sea Scrolls. The second movement, located in the cities and in the countryside, was originated by the Pharisees. Jesus was close to them. During the Middle Ages, *havurot*, groups of men or "brotherhoods" devoted to prayer and common study, appeared in many Jewish communities; they were devoted to study and mystical speculation. A later development, in the eighteenth century, was the *Chevra* (brotherhood), which served the spiritual and economic needs of its members. The Hasidic movement gave new strength to the movement.

Neuhaus: What about the American experience?

Klenicki: The first evidence of Havurah institutional commitment appeared in the early sixties with a publication of an issue of *The Reconstructionist*, which outlined the idea of Havurah and encouraged its development. The Jewish Reconstructionist Movement was very much interested in following the ideas of Mordecai Kaplan, a twentieth-century American Jewish theologian. He considered Judaism an evolving civilization, stressing the creative diversity of Jewish thought and practices.

Neuhaus: Perhaps you should say something about the theology behind the movement.

Klenicki: Havurah is involved with an ongoing religious quest, rooted in traditional forms of Judaism, but open to experimentation and adaptation. The search is for meaningful liturgies, the companionship of the membership in a sort of extended family, and the social activities that cooperate in the realization of the kingdom of God.

Havurah can be part of a synagogue, a community center, or the action of a group of academicians meeting in houses or at a university facility. In many cases it is a surrogate synagogue.

Neuhaus: Do you think this search for relevance, as you put it, makes a difference to the individual Jew and the community?

Klenicki: Havurah essentially is to live a Jewish existence regulated by a sense of daily performance of the covenant with God. It is the wish to live with spiritual security related to an actualization of tradition. Tradition is understood in Max Weber's observation as "the authority of eternal history." The thirst for tradition is manifested in the success of the *Jewish Catalog.* The first edition came out in 1973 and has almost achieved the status of a "sacred text." Yes, it makes a difference.

Havurah fosters a Jewish life experience expressed in prayer, study, joint communal meals on Friday nights, the keeping of kashrut and the Sabbath, wearing yarmulkes, and so on.

This aspect of religious existence, of accepting God in daily life, is taken as the means to express the covenant, not as an end in itself. There is a gradual acceptance of the duties of religiosity, an acceptance of rules beyond the fear of divine punishment for not keeping a rule, as it occurs in traditional "medieval" understandings. It is a celebration of the joy of being religious.

That is what I am trying to teach my children, and to project to them: I am Jewish, I try to live my covenant with God in every moment of my life, and the life of my family. I wear my yarmulke openly. Before, I would use it only for praying or at meals; now I go everywhere covered. It is a sign of my own growth in recognizing God as central in my everyday life and the life of my family. It is also a challenge. It is easy to wear a yarmulke in the U.S.A., yet quite strange to do it in other countries. It can even be a personal trial in Poland. I remember visiting Warsaw, walking on the streets that knew an active Jewish life forty years ago. I remember Poles looking at me; I can still see the surprise in their eyes. Or when I am in Argentina, I can feel curiosity—often friendly curiosity, but also hostility.

This is the challenge: to be religious in what you have called "the naked public square." To be religious *and* American, and to work to apply religious life and values to national life.

Haunted by the Past

Neuhaus: And so, as you say, this rethinking of the linkage between Judaism and secularization is in its beginning stages, especially as it relates to public policy and how we ought to order our life together in society.

Klenicki: But, Richard, let me interrupt and express another of our fears and trembling. Whenever we think in terms of projecting religious life into the public arena, we are reminded of past experiences.

Neuhaus: Of course.

Klenicki: We remember religious persecution in the Middle Ages, and the political games of Christian groups in the United States and elsewhere. In Latin America, for example, the right-wing Catholic groups are denying basic rights to minorities.

Neuhaus: It is very important, Leon, and it is important to understand that this is not just a Jewish anxiety. It has to be an anxiety of anyone who cares about the future of this kind of society—a democratic, pluralistic, constitutional republic. The answer to the naked public square, as I keep trying to make clear, is not just more religion in public. More religion in public could be very bad, bad not only for minorities—in this case, Jews in America—but also for our understanding of our social and political order. The question is: What kind of religion is going to go public? What we need is a religiously grounded understanding of the moral legitimations, the moral warrants and imperatives, of a pluralistic and democratic society. And I have to admit that this rethinking of the connection between religion and the public square, which as you have said is just beginning in the Jewish community, is just beginning in the Christian community as well. And it must also be admitted that some of the Christian forces which are most militantly opposed to what they call secular humanism, and which are most eager to assert religiously based truth claims in the public arena, have not thought through the theological rationale for a free and democratic society. So Christians and Jews need to be engaged in dialogue with regard to the civil order, as well as with regard to the much more important question of our covenantal relationship.

But now we are in danger of forgetting the question that one or both of us raised earlier: Why is it that the Jews who seem to be most religiously Jewish seem also to be most reluctant to enter into dialogue of a theological or spiritual nature?

Klenicki: I would say again that it has to do with our historical experience. Every time I talk about the theological conversations I have had with Christians, my more traditional Jewish friends say that we have no theology in Judaism, or that theological discussions will only lead to confrontation, as they did in past, or to syncretism. They recommend that we should avoid theology and deal only with social problems. But I point out to them that even in the consideration of social problems—such as the question of poverty, for example, or the future of the human being in the nuclear era—we do theology. If I try to analyze the nature of the human being, I base my examination not in Marxism or ideology but in the Bible, the Talmud, and Jewish religious thought. My analysis comes out of my tradition, a natural development that some find difficult to accept. Perhaps we are not yet ready or prepared for the challenge of interfaith theological discussion. Past confrontation is still lingering in our collective memory.

The orthodox community's negative attitude toward theological dialogue also relates to a distrust of the surrounding society. We have had sad experiences in the past, both in medieval Western Europe and in the contemporary scene. It is possible that some theological discussion between Jews and Christians took place in prewar Europe, but nothing like what is now possible in the atmosphere of our American pluralism. Europe has never been pluralistic. In Germany, for example, there was some tolerance after the First World War, expressed in the discussions between Martin Buber and contemporary Christian thinkers, but it never became a real dialogue. Significant progress was made in the next few years, however. Rabbi Leo Baeck, for example, a great spiritual leader, paid much attention to an understanding of the New Testament and Jesus as they relate to the Jewish-Christian dialogue.

I can understand the distrustful feelings of my most

traditional friends, but I remind them that we live in the U.S.A., a pluralistic society. This pluralism gives us the opportunity to talk or not to talk, to relate or not to relate to Christians. It also gives us the unique possibility of living out our Jewish covenant and our relationship with God totally and openly, along with Christians who are going through the same experience vis-à-vis their commitment.

Neuhaus: Yes, we have mentioned before the distinctiveness of the American situation for Jewish-Christian encounter. I do not think it is too much to say that there is something providential in this situation. If we could project ourselves a hundred or five hundred years into the future, I believe we could look back at this moment of Jewish-Christian dialogue in America and recognize it as a positive turning point in the relationship between Christians and Jews. If that is true, then looking back from the end of history, so to speak, we would see this as a moment of God's work in which he helped us, Jews and Christians alike, to more fully understand the redemptive purpose of which we are both a part.

A Deeper Dialogue

Klenicki: I agree with you completely. There are, however, two conditions attached to your hope of a joint work of redemption. One is the internal and the external acceptance of our missions. We Jews believe that we have been chosen for the specific task of witnessing God in daily life and history. We have been chosen for a mission. But for many Jews this is difficult to accept because they fear that others will see us as trying to appear superior, better than others. For centuries we have been accused of that. As a result, many Jews have given up this mission. It is a hard task, an awesome daily obligation of being a partner of God. Can Christians accept our special role as God's chosen people? Can we Jews accept it internally and then express it externally in communion with humanity?

The other condition for a joint testimony of redemption is our own understanding of Christianity and its role or vocation in the world. Is the only vocation of Christians to be our oppressors for centuries? Are you also God's messengers to the world? What is Jesus' role in God's design? I doubt if it would be possible to ask these questions outside the reality of American pluralism. To resolve these questions we need the security of freedom to exercise our own spirituality, as well as the security of being accepted as we are—a people chosen by God with a specific mission, with an eternal covenant—and not as just the prelude to another mission, or fulfilled by another religious commitment.

Neuhaus: There are uncertainties about the dialogue all around. For instance, Christians often complain about what they see as the one-sidedness of the dialogue. And here I have to say that there are things that Christians say to Christians that they do not usually say to the Jews in these dialogues.

Klenicki: And vice versa.

Neuhaus: On this matter of one-sidedness, the complaint goes like this: "The Jews expect us to come in and confess our manifold sins against them, whereas they

50

confess no sins of their own. They expect us to learn their vocabulary, and their way of thinking, but they frequently do not even make an effort to learn the basics of Christian theology or belief or practice." And so the general allegation is that there is an asymmetry in the dialogue—an asymmetry of guilt, of obligation, and of effort. I can understand this, but I think the Christians who make this complaint fail to appreciate the degree of insecurity on the Jewish side, an insecurity horrendously warranted by the experience of centuries. In saying that, I am not engaging in a ritual of Christian self-denigration. This history is a fact with which we must cope. The dialogue does not begin now from scratch, as though we were writing on a tabula rasa. If historians want to point out that in the early centuries there were many instances in which Jews made Christians feel very insecure, that is fine. Indeed, it is very important to an understanding of the complexity of our connection. But it is true that the historical causes of Jewish insecurity are much more numerous and more depressing.

I believe that Christians who complain that the burden of learning and being sensitive is one-sided are often speaking out of a very early experience with the dialogue. That is to say, once the securities, the mutual securities, are in place, the conversation takes a quite different form. Certainly this is true in our conversation, and I am glad to say that in this respect Leon Klenicki is not alone among Jews in the dialogue. But Christians do need to encounter people like you who are studying Paul's Epistle to the Romans, who are entering enough into an understanding of the Christian reality so that you can challenge Christians on their own terms, so to speak, just as Christians can likewise put Jewish questions to Jews. There is a sense in which we put ourselves at risk here, and that can sometimes make us very ner-

51

vous. But it is of the essence of interreligious dialogue, I believe, that we determinedly make ourselves vulnerable to the other. Of course, that must go hand in hand with a growth in mutual trust, trust which can only come from the experience of dialogue, and which makes it possible for us to take the risk.

This matter of trust raises another question concerning the traditionalist hesitancy about theological dialogue, which you mentioned earlier. Many Americans are very much aware of those Jews who are called the Hasidim and who live in places such as Williamsburg and Crown Heights in Brooklyn, perhaps because their communities are so colorful. Their eighteenth-century European clothing, close-knit communities, and rigorous observance of religious rites and practices make them stand out. To many Christians, and perhaps even to many Jews, they seem like "the real Jews," the genuine article. I have heard, also from Jews, different evaluations of their significance, and perhaps you could say something about this. One interpretation is that these people are in fact very inadequate Jews because they are running away from the Jewish obligation to the nations. They are involved, it is said, in a process of self-ghettoization in which they have abandoned the mission of Israel. The other and sharply different view is that they have read the Jewish situation correctly. They understand that Judaism is in such crisis because of unbelief and the ravages of secularization, and therefore that their kind of community, which looks like self-ghettoization, is in fact imperative. It is, if you will, a holding action, an attempt to inoculate at least a segment of Judaism against the disease of modernity. Maybe somewhere down the historical turnpike, it is said, the time will come when the more universal mission of Israel can be resumed.

I confess that I have something of a personal interest in this. As you know, for many years I was pastor of a black parish in Brooklyn located right next to the Hasidic community in Williamsburg. There were all kinds of tensions, of course, and I had very ambivalent feelings about the Hasidim. I recall talking to Heschel once about the admirable familial and spiritual solidarity of the Hasidim, and he strongly suggested that I was indulging in romanticism. Of course, his own family lineage, going back several generations, was Hasidic in Poland. But what is your own thinking when you look at the Jews of Williamsburg or Crown Heights?

Klenicki: I feel great sympathy for their experience of God, though I, personally, cannot share their way of living. I like to go to Hasidic services, listen to their interpretation of the Hebrew Bible, and sense the presence of God in their midst, but I cannot live in their way. I respect them, but I also . . .

Neuhaus: Why not? Why can you not?

Klenicki: Because I am the product of Western Europe and Western culture. The Hasidim relate to a certain moment of history. In many respects they are still living in the eighteenth century, while I am a product of the twentieth century, approaching the twenty-first. It's not that my time is better than theirs, though my experience is different. What I want is to share the feeling of God, each one in his own way, and also to share the reality of Jewish covenantal life, according to personal experience and perspectives. There is no one way. There is a pluralism of ways of living God's experience and the covenant with God. I am not defending modernity; I am endorsing the right to be different in the Jewish religious pursuit, the right to maintain pluralism in Jewish religious life.

53

"Authentic" Religion

Neuhaus: Leon, let me play devil's advocate for a moment, because I think there are things we Christians need to understand. How would you respond if someone said, "Well now, what you're really saying, Rabbi Klenicki, is that you are not as radically religious a Jew as the Hasidim are. When you say you cannot live that way, you are in fact admitting that you are not as full-hearted a Jew. If you were a more thoroughgoing Jew, you would be prepared to dismiss the twentieth century and to live unqualifiedly by Jewish identity as represented, for instance, by the Hasidim of Williamsburg." I need not tell you that there are in fact Jews in Williamsburg who would challenge you in those terms. So how do you respond?

Klenicki: I would say that even if this were the eighteenth century, I do not know if I would be part of the Hasidic movement. I would be part of the Orthodox community, emphasizing the rule of *Halakah* and the implementation of God's covenant in everyday life, but I have great doubt that I would follow the Hasidic life. What I want to emphasize again is that there must be pluralism of religious expressions in Judaism.

I fear it when one group within Judaism wants to impose their values upon everyone, as certain fanatic groups are now doing in Israel, imposing their fundamentalism on the rest of the population. That I cannot accept. I want a Jewish milieu in which I can live my own religious life, just as the Hasidim live in their religious way. I have great respect for Hasidism from what I consider my conservative religious position. I am respectful of their way, but I am also asking them to have respect for my search for a living God.

Neuhaus: Of course, there are Christian analogies here. That is to say, there are Christians who assert that authentic Christianity, radical Christianity, requires a wholesale rejection of the modern world. I do not have in mind so much the monastic movement as self-styled radical Christians who tend to set themselves up as the norm of true discipleship, which they believe calls for a studied indifference—even hostility—to the culture of which we are part. Again, one must say that there is much that is admirable in that, but at the same time I think that both of us would be compelled to say that to deny that we are twentieth-century, post-Enlightenment human beings would in fact be a course of unfaithfulness. For Christians too, this business of religious identity and cultural participation, of setting ourselves against the culture and of trying to shape the culture, is painfully complicated. We say we must be *in* the world but not *of* the world, and just when we think we've gotten the hang of living that way, the situation changes and we have to start all over again. Embattled sect, triumphant Christendom, self-conscious counter-culture—we have been all of those and more, and it is hard to say which is the "authentic" Christian way.

We do not live in the first century, or the eighteenth, or the twelfth, but rather on the edge of the twenty-first. While trying to respect people who think that they can create or recreate a moment of the past in which they can celebrate what they view as authentic religion, I would say with you that that is not my vocation. I would be disobedient to what I understand to be my calling from God if I did not to try to exercise—as best I can— what it means to be faithful, what it means to believe, in this historical moment.

Klenicki: Richard, your point is well taken. In certain traditional circles, the denial of the twentieth century seems to be a denial of creation. The twentieth century is part of the creation history and part of our contribution. So, if I am denying this time, I am also denying the very fact of creation. I would also point out that the dress of Hasidic men relates more to the fashion of the eighteenth century than to Moses' time. Would Moses dress like that in the hot weather of the land of Israel? I doubt that very much.

Neuhaus: And one must raise the question, why is it more sanctified to adopt the worldly dress of the eighteenth century than the worldly dress of the twentieth century?

Klenicki: Exactly. But of course, in their defense, one could point out the lax standards of dress in our time, much more lax today than they were in the eighteenth century.

Neuhaus: To be sure, there is a long list of reasons for being powerfully ambivalent about our historical moment. This has been, after all, the bloodiest of human centuries, in which human madnesses have piled up corpses beyond numbering and produced rivers of blood. One can mention Stalin, the Gulag Archipelago, Chairman Mao and the cultural revolution, and on and on. But in connection with our subject, we think most particularly of the Holocaust under the Third Reich. There is no end of reflection on the Holocaust, for it suggests so much about the modernity project and what we persist in calling Western civilization. But it is also an event of theological importance that some Christians do not hesitate to compare with the crucifixion.

Klenicki: Indeed. For the Jewish people and for Judaism itself, this is a turning point in our history, a turning point in our witnessing God. It is also a recognition of our disillusion with European toleration and the hopes and dreams of the Enlightenment. Toleration was a philosophy and a system that made us believe that we were accepted in European society. In reality we were just tolerated and never accepted. The Holocaust ended that situation. It marks a time of total exile, and it serves as a reminder of other such moments in our history: for example, the Exodus story, the slavery in Egypt, and the return to the Promised Land; the destruction of the First Temple; the exile to Babylon and the return to the Promised Land; the destruction of the Second Temple in the year 70 and the subsequent rebuilding of Jewish spiritual life, the building of the temple inside the heart of Judaism which was done by the Pharisaic and rabbinic schools.

Neuhaus: The inner temple.

Klenicki: Yes. The inner temple of Judaism was the consequence of the destruction of the physical body of the temple. As you can see, there is a constant theme of exile and return in our history. Sometimes—in the Babylonian exile, for example—our prophets and rabbis would point out that God used the Babylonians to punish the infidelity of Judaism and the Jewish people. But vis-à-vis our experience of the Holocaust, it is impossible for me, and for my community in general, to think that this too was God's punishment of the Jewish people. I cannot accept that God would send punishment in the form of the death of one child: how much more unacceptable it would be in the form of the one million children gassed in the concentration camps. I cannot think in those terms. Instead, I try to explain the Holocaust in terms of another dimension. For me, Nazism is the total triumph of the evil inclination of the human being. Rabbinic theology says that at creation, man was provided with two tendencies: the tendency toward good and the tendency toward evil. People have to balance those two powers in themselves and to try to live the covenant in their daily existence through stressing, building up, and enriching the strength of the good inclination. Under Nazism, the evil inclination was totally triumphant. It nearly reached a victory in trying to destroy the people of God, which is essentially the attempt to destroy God. In a parallel example, I would say that Stalin's attempt to destroy religion, condemning religious people, is essentially a pagan attempt to destroy Judaism and Christianity.

Concern for Jews as Jews

Neuhaus: Yes, such interpretations underscore the human capacity for radical evil. There is another interpretation, however, about which we should at least say something. As you know, there are those who claim that the Holocaust was really the final and logical working out of Christian anti-Semitism. One hears, from both Christians and Jews, that Christianity is inherently and irredeemably anti-Semitic. There is, for example, the famous—or infamous—statement by a noted rabbi: "What was started at the Council of Nicea was duly completed in the concentration camps and crematoria of the Third Reich." Then too, at the very heart of Hitler's darkness, yet another interpretation was set forth. We are told that many Jews went to their deaths accepting them as the just punishment of Israel's infidelities.

These and other interpretations continue to pose

problems in the dialogue. Not long ago there was considerable controversy over John Cardinal O'Connor's visit to the Holocaust museum in Jerusalem. You will recall that he was deeply moved and compared that suffering to that of Christ on the cross, suggesting that the suffering of the Jews was somehow a gift to humanity. There were many protests, in both the religious and the general media, against what was viewed as a desecration, almost an obscenity, against the memory of the six million dead, but these people had no understanding of what Cardinal O'Connor meant by redemptive suffering. And this is only one example of the problems we have in sorting out "the lessons" of the Holocaust. We talk about the lessons we learn from history, and there are endless arguments about the "lessons of Vietnam" or the "lessons of Munich," but nowhere is that argument so intense as it is over the lessons of the Holocaust.

In this connection, what you said about the barbarity of Stalin and the Gulag also needs to be emphasized more in relation to the Holocaust. Both are instances of the intense concentration of humanity's cosmic rebellion against God. Living Judaism was the icon of God in the eyes of the enemies of God. This is not to deny in any way that Nazism was also an anti-Christian movement. But it must be said, to the great shame of us Christians, that with relatively few exceptions, the Christians of Germany, both Lutheran and Roman Catholic, did not permit themselves to "stick out," in the way that Jews had no choice but to stick out, against the totalitarian designs of the Nazi regime. Indeed, had the church been the Church, had it been more true to its vocation to be an icon of God in history, the devastating, demonic winds of the Holocaust would undoubtedly have been directed at the church, just as they were directed at Judaism. We now know that Hitler had long-term but definite plans for the destruction of the Church as well. And we must avoid self-righteousness on this subject, for who knows what we would have done if we had been in the position of the Christians of Germany? But we know what we hope we would have done, and we know what in fact most Christians did, and the memory of that must continue to trouble us deeply.

Klenicki: In this respect, it is important to reflect upon the attitude of the great Lutheran theologian Dietrich Bonhoeffer. After the passage of the Nuremberg Laws, he criticized the Nazi ideology, but only with regard to those Jews who had converted to Christianity. His only concern was this: What was their position as converts vis-à-vis the Nuremberg Laws? This is a sad matter, and such indifference to Jewish destiny makes it difficult to continue reading him. I pointed out this matter to his biographer, his brother-in-law, Eberhard Bethge.

We had a long conversation, and when I pointed out this issue he was surprised. Later on, he wrote an article about it, showing that Bonhoeffer later realized the mistake he had made in the early thirties.

I would like to clarify one matter that you referred to before: I would not accept the statement that the main promoter of the Shoah, or the Holocaust, was Christianity and the Christian churches. I would like to stress, however, that the two thousand years of the Christian teaching of contempt for Jews and Judaism and the denial of the Jewish vocation of God did influence and help Hitler in his plan. There was a European framework of viewing Jews and Judaism as second-class people, often pictured in art and literature. Jews lived in separate quarters and had no civil rights; only in the nineteenth century were they admitted as full-fledged citizens, and even then with certain limitations. So, indirectly, Christian thought and the teaching of contempt were working and were active in the Nazi ideology, though Nazism—I repeat it once again—was a pagan movement. It had nothing to do with Christian faith, though the Nazis may have used aspects of Christianity for their own ideological reasons.

Neuhaus: Yes. And at the same time one must reject the statement cited earlier, that the Holocaust was the fulfillment of Nicea and of Christian orthodoxy, which is inherently anti-Semitic. I take that to be an outrageous slander and simply a misreading of history, and I regret that some Christians think that they are advancing understanding between Christians and Jews when they go along with such a malicious proposition. Some years ago Milton Himmelfarb wrote an important article refuting this belief, "No Hitler, No Holocaust," in which he argued that Hitler was not a product of Christian anti-Semitism but rather was the determined enemy of Judaism and Christianity alike. While I agree with that, I do not at all discount Christian culpability in "the teaching of contempt," which certainly made Hitler's work easier.

To Be a Victim

Klenicki: Exactly. I am sorry for interrupting you, Richard. There were many, many Christian prisoners in Auschwitz, both lay people and clergy.

Neuhaus: Yes, there was opposition to the regime. There were the Dietrich Bonhoeffers, and there was the Confessing Church that based itself on the Barmen Declaration of 1934. But there was also so much else.

On the question of the Holocaust, Leon, and precisely for the sake of the dialogue, let me elicit your response to some issues raised by many Christians. It seems to some people that there is no end of books, articles, television series, and so forth on the Holocaust. I have had Christians say to me, "Enough already!" There is this feeling that it is being overdone, that we are always being hit over the head with the Holocaust. It is hard to know how to respond to this. If people feel they are simply sated with the story, or that they are not emotionally prepared to go through the anguish of it all again, well, that is one thing. But there is another kind of argument being made when people protest that "the Jews have no monopoly on suffering."

There are subtleties at work here. Deeply entrenched in our culture, and it undoubtedly has roots in biblical thought, is this matter of the moral status of the victim. We have seen it at work in black-white relations for many decades. Some social critics have written about the need to "achieve" victim status in order to occupy the moral high ground in relation to other groups. Needless to say, this is much resented by some in the other groups. Thus with respect to the Holocaust, we hear Christians say that, yes, it was a terrible thing that has happened in history. But Eastern Orthodox Christians—Armenians, Ukrainians, Russians—ask why so much is made of six million Jews while so little public attention is paid the fifty million Christians who perished under Stalin. And of course there is a particular complaint from Polish Christians who suffered unspeakably under the Nazis, and from Slavs generally, whom Hitler scheduled for another "final solution."

Well, you are familiar with this line of objection. As obligated as Jews are to remember their victims, these

Christians feel obligated to remember theirs. "Attention must be paid," as Willy Loman's wife says in *Death of a Salesman*. And attention is paid in some observances of the Holocaust in synagogues around the country. There is the practice, for instance, of lighting six candles for the Jewish victims and five, or maybe six, for the Christians. The point is—and this is to put a positive interpretation on it—that there is a desire to internalize the Holocaust as a human tragedy, and more particularly as a tragedy for the people of the covenant, both Jewish and Christian. It is not, people want to insist, just the horror story of one group. One can understand that.

And yet, and yet, surely we should remember the Christian victims, and those who are called "the righteous Gentiles" who, with astonishing heroism, saved hundreds of thousands of Jewish lives. All of that having been said, we Christians must nonetheless recognize the truth of what you say. I would only, in passing, amend your statement that Nazism was a pagan movement. Paganism at its best possessed a measure of human dignity. Paganism would have been a move up for the Nazis. Nazism was a barbarian force directed against Judaism, Christianity, and every other civilizing influence. At the same time, Christians do bear a large measure of responsibility for helping to create a cultural climate in which that barbarian force was released, in which even the anti-Christian impulse could be effectively politicized and finally implemented as policy by a demonic regime.

There is a certain ambiguity even about those who resisted. You earlier spoke a hard truth about Pastor Dietrich Bonhoeffer. He was a giant among men and, I believe, a saint. Incidentally, in the calendar of the *Lutheran Book of Worship*, the day of his execution— April 9—is noted, but he is described simply as "teacher." It should also say "martyr," for he surely was that. Granted all that, however, some of what he wrote about the Jews is deeply flawed. The same must be said about another very major figure, Paul Tillich. In 1934, Emanuel Hirsch, a German theologian of great stature and a very close friend of Tillich, had become an apologist for the Nazis. He wrote what we would today call a liberation theology, a political theology legitimizing the National Socialist revolution. Tillich, who had by then been exiled to the United States, wrote a long, troubled, and sharply critical letter to Hirsch. It is a very moving letter, but it is also very depressing in one respect. When it comes to "the Jewish question," Tillich criticizes Hirsch for giving priority to the blood-and-soil ideology of National Socialism over the solidarity of Christians and Jews in the eucharistic body and blood of Christ. In other words, and as in the case of Bonhoeffer, the stated concern was for Jewish Christians, not for Jews as such. It should be said in fairness that this thirty-page letter does not by a long shot contain everything that Tillich said about Jews and Judaism. But it is noteworthy that, in this critical appeal to Hirsch, the suggestion is that Jews are incorporated into the circle of Christian moral responsibility only to the degree to which they had become Christian.

Klenicki: Richard, I am grateful for what you just said, because one of our concerns is the tendency to universalize the Holocaust, and even to Christianize the Holocaust, by putting aside the drama of the Jewish people.

I have the warmest affection for Cardinal O'Connor and respect the sincerity of his love for the Jewish people and Judaism. I've told him personally, however, that I have serious reservations about the Holocaust being compared with the cross of Christ. I can understand the Christian attempt to see an event in terms of their own commitment, but I also feel that such analogies diminish the essential Jewish meaning of the event. John Paul II expressed this in his Miami speech to the Jewish leadership when he described the Holocaust as "the death of the Jewish people," avoiding any descriptive Christian image.

The word "holocaust" has been used and abused in describing the situation of women, the abortion question, and the reality of blacks in the U.S.A. "Holocaust" has been used to describe any human situation. Such indiscriminate use of this term diminishes the original sense of the word. Are we denied our own martyrdom?

Millions perished under Nazi occupation. Poles and Russians were second in the line of destruction but they were victims by chance, caught by the SS or the Gestapo and sent to concentration camps. There was no special ideology for their destruction. But the Jews were victims by birth: to be Jewish meant to be destined to destruction. While other people could choose either going into hiding or joining the guerrilla forces, for the Jews there were very few opportunities of that kind, or none at all. I am awed by the cases of non-Jews who chose to give their lives for a prisoner—Maximilian Kolbe in Auschwitz, for example. But Jews did not have the opportunity for any choice; they were condemned from the very beginning. And there are even ambiguities surrounding some of these figures, such as Father Kolbe.

Kolbe, before the war, was the general editor of a publishing company which produced many Catholic publications, among them one of the most anti-Semitic publications in Poland. I find it very ironic that this man—who might have agreed with that publication, since he was the general editor of the company that published it—suffered personally what the magazine was demanding—namely, the destruction of the Jewish people. He could see it every day in Auschwitz. How valuable it would be to know what his reflections were on the human Jewish situation and the Christian teaching of contempt while he was himself in Auschwitz!

We also have great difficulties with the case of the beatification of Edith Stein. Sister Stein didn't die because she was a Catholic nun. Conversion to Christianity did not assure being saved from the Nazis. They sent committed Jews, indifferent Jews, and converted Jews to the gas chambers. I wonder how Sister Stein is considered by her fellow Catholics. In the speech that John Paul II gave on the occasion of her beatification, he referred constantly to her Jewishness, projecting the idea that her conversion to Christianity was the fulfillment of her Judaism. But I don't know how Jewish she was in her youth. From what I have read, she was rather indifferent, or knew very litle about the Jewish tradition. How could she be fulfilled in something she didn't know much about?

Neuhaus: Well, as I said earlier, Leon, we and generations to come will likely be sorting out these painful questions which place enormous strain on Jewish-Christian relations. Those of us who are pledged to what has been said about the providential purpose of the dialogue have a particular responsibility to address these questions with all the candor and all the sensitivity that we can muster. On some of these questions, I confess to a deep ambivalence. I think I understand why some Jews are so worried about universalizing, or "de-Judaizing," the Shoah. And that must be a concern of Christians as well, that we do not abstract the Holocaust from the historical particularity that is Living Judaism as an icon of God's covenantal fidelity.

Mainly because of the enormous effort of Jewish writers, thinkers, and communicators, the Shoah has been etched—one hopes indelibly etched—in the consciousness of our culture. The reality has been, as they say, inculturated. But this also means that it is no longer the story of just one group—namely, the Jews. If it is viewed in that way, it simply becomes one great tragedy among others. In that case, all other victimized groups—the Cambodians, Ukrainians, Armenians, and on and on—understandably clamor for "equal time." To be sure, each of these stories should also be inculturated, should be recognized as *our* story. But we must avoid playing horror stories off against each other. That is not only unseemly with respect to the memory of the dead, but it also trivializes the horror by reducing it to a rivalry among tribalisms. For many reasons, no story has been so culturally internalized as that of the Holocaust. Its being internalized by people who are not Jews does not make it any less Jewish, but it does mean that other people—Christians, for example—will also speak of it in their own way. Here again, the instance of Cardinal O'Connor in Jerusalem is instructive. If we Christians are to speak "Christianly" about the Holocaust, it is to be expected that our speaking will engage the image of the cross. The cross is for us the paradigm of redemptive suffering, and of God's fidelity despite the worst that can possibly happen.

On some of these questions, I expect many Christians and Jews will continue to disagree, at least for a time, until we sort them out better. You mention the beatification of Edith Stein, for example, and how many Jews were troubled by that. It is true that the Nazis sent her to the concentration camp and killed her because she was Jewish, not because she was a Christian nun of saintly stature. But then one must ask this question: What did *she* understand to be the meaning of her death? The answer seems to be clear. She believed she was offering up her life in communion with the crucified Lord. So whose interpretation of this event should prevail? Surely her own interpretation has a privileged status, or so it seems to me. As a matter of historical fact, she was killed because she was Jewish. There is no doubt about that. Equally, there is no doubt that she affirmed the church's interpretation of her death as an instance of Christian martyrdom. And my hunch is that, if we were to explore this yet more deeply, we would discover that those interpretations are not mutually exclusive, but complementary.

But this is only one example of a larger set of questions. These questions may well increase as more people and different people become involved in drawing "the lessons of the Holocaust." We can expect controversies over interpretation, over what might be called the hermeneutics of the Holocaust. I don't think we should be surprised by that.

Klenicki: No, we are not surprised by that. I would say that, in our passionate, negative response to the tendency to describe the Holocaust in Christian terms, we are expressing our fear of a tendency to Christianize an event that was—and is—essentially Jewish. But there is also the awesome fact that we ourselves do not want to go into the very recondite meaning of the Holocaust, that is, to go beyond the description of the horror in order to understand its significance and formulate a response, to put the Holocaust in its theological and historical perspective. In the course of Jewish history, we have experienced many moments of exile and return to God. We tried on each occasion to reflect on God's call and its new meanings. After the Babylonian exile, for example, as it is stated in Nehemiah 8, Ezra brought out a scroll—we know now that it was probably the book of Deuteronomy—to read and comment on. Ezra, in front of all of the people in Jerusalem, explained the meaning of the text and started the rabbinic movement that expounded the meaning of the biblical word of God as a response to history.

68

I feel this is another moment like that. It is another turning point in our history when we have the sacred duty to think beyond horror. But the memory of the concentration camps hurts deeply. Beyond horror, what is the meaning of the covenant with God after Auschwitz? Why was God apparently silent, and how do I testify to the covenant, my relationship with God, in this time of history and for the next century?

No Posthumous Victories

Neuhaus: These are awesome questions and, as you say, they will continue to be pondered also by generations to come. But perhaps you share with me a certain ambivalence about some of the ways in which the Shoah is theologized. One thinks, for example, of Richard Rubenstein, who, if I understand him, argues that the Holocaust means the end of theology, the end of meaningful talk about God.

Klenicki: I'm afraid that his approach is more emotional than rational.

Neuhaus: Perhaps so. What I was getting at is that marvelous statement by Emil Fackenheim that we must not grant Hitler any posthumous victories. And one posthumous victory that Jews and Christians must not grant Hitler is the idea that there can be such horror as to eliminate the mercy of God. I am thinking of the words of David Novak who recently wrote that, as a Jew, he begins the day by praising God, not by cursing Hitler.

You recall that in the 1960s a number of Jewish and Christian theologians were involved in what was called "death of God" theology. I remember Heschel poignantly inquiring about what they could possibly mean. "Certainly talk about the death of God can only mean the death of man," Heschel said. In any event, the Holocaust played a prominent part in the thinking of these people, and, without impugning motives, I am afraid that some of them drew conclusions that might be described as posthumous victories for Hitler. We Jews and Christians are called, I think, not to tell the Holocaust story, whether theologically or otherwise, in a way that serves the forces of darkness.

Klenicki: It is also a call to commitment, commitment to our own faith and beliefs and also to a sense of responsibility for the young. Just a few months ago I was in Poland, and I visited the site of the Auschwitz concentration camp where all my family, with the exception of one uncle, perished.

Neuhaus: This was your first time?

Klenicki: That was my first visit to Poland and Auschwitz. For years I had told myself that I had to go and visit Auschwitz, I had to say *Kaddish*, the prayer for the departed, for my family and for my people who were exterminated there. Both emotionally and spiritually, it was not easy to go into that place, or even to come near the site of the concentration camp. I remember that the taxi driver who took me to Auschwitz from Krakow said to me, "I won't go with you. I let you out here. I was here once. I don't want to go into that place again." The man was born long after the war. He was a very young person. And there I was walking through Auschwitz, and I broke down several times because I realized that this was the place where my family walked to the very end of their lives. One day they disappeared here—when, on the day of their arrival, Mengele assigned who would go to the right, to a life in the daily agony of the concentration camp, or to the left, to death, to the gas chambers.

And then I walked down to the gas chambers. I have to tell you, Richard, I couldn't say a word. I couldn't pray. I was in awe, shaken and in tears. I made myself go back to the prayer book and pray the *Kaddish.* I told myself that I had to say that prayer. I had to say that. I did it in tears.

When I was walking through the different buildings, I realized that the Communist government has taken out any reference to the Jewish people and their destruction. There is practically no reference to the fact that nearly three and a half million Jews were killed in Auschwitz. Nothing. There are references to all other nationalities, but no reference to the Jewish people. This is so significant that when John Paul II visited Auschwitz, he looked for the plate in Hebrew that describes the concentration camp but does not say anything about the Jews who died there. For this reason, the pope deliberately mentioned that Jews died in Auschwitz, as a message for his fellow Poles and also for the Communist government.

While I was walking, a painful thought came upon me: How is such an evil possible? How is it possible that a person would send children six or eight years old—the age of my cousins—to the gas chambers, knowing that they would die in a few seconds? How can a mind be so diabolically perverse? Then immediately another case came to my mind, the case of Argentina. I thought about Argentina during the rule of the generals after 1976, when hundreds of people disappeared or were killed, tortured to death in a horrible manner. The justification was a "dirty war" against Marxism. The generals did not bring people to trial, but they just murdered them. I visited Buenos Aires to lecture and express my concern about the situation in the country. I talked to Jews and Christians, clergy, bishops, and even generals. The response was always the same: "That's Marxist propaganda." I never heard anybody say, "Yes, you are right, this is happening in our country. What should we do about it?" Religious and spiritual leaders could have spoken; there was more freedom under the generals than under the Nazis. Why was this evil accepted by religious people? I feel very sad about the fact that the religious leadership, with few exceptions, did not denounce such an evil in Argentina.

Neuhaus: It has often been said, with some justice, that original sin is the only biblical doctrine that can be empirically proved beyond reasonable doubt. In connection with the Holocaust, Hannah Arendt spoke about the banality of evil, but there is also something perversely exquisite in the consummation of the human capacity for evil. It may be banal in the manner of its day-by-day implementation, but the impulse—the drive—to evil is not banal by any means. It is not alarmist to say that it could happen again. We so earnestly declare "Never again!" precisely because we are aware that it could happen again. It's not alarmist to say that it could happen here. Of course, "it" would take a peculiarly American form, but that makes the prospect no less ominous. Among the less attractive American conceits is the notion that we are a virtuous people without such capacity for radical evil.

Klenicki: And for that reason, I would say that Auschwitz obligates us Jews and Christians to go beyond recrimination. We should try to understand that we have a joint mission vis-à-vis Auschwitz—that is, to exercise our covenants, our relationship with God, and to implement it in our common fight against the evil diabolical tendencies in human beings. This is a must in our relationship: to witness God and to denounce evil.

Selective Justice

Neuhaus: Right, but discerning evil and contending against it does not come easily for many of us. The Christian record on this score has not always been very impressive, to put it mildly. One thinks of the 1930s, both in Germany and here in America, when we had a truly diabolical sentimentalism on the part of most Christians, who simply refused to recognize the reality of evil. That was the kind of sentimentalism which Reinhold Niebuhr and others had to fight against so vigorously. In the culture, and very strongly in the churches, we had this dominant idea that what Stalin was doing was really not so bad, and what Hitler was doing was really not so bad. The sentimental doctrine was that, if only we understood one another better, then we could build a more constructive relationship on mutual trust. And so, in this process of well-intended self-delusion, these sentimentalists became, in fact, apologists for oppression.

And, sad to say, this continues to happen today. One thinks of the compelling witness of Armando Valladares, who for more than twenty years was jailed and tortured for his faith in Cuba. In his book *Against All Hope*, he describes how the Christian prisoners derived comfort from the belief that Christians in America and

elsewhere were praying for them, but then, when dele-
gations of American religious leaders would come to
Cuba, they would downplay or even deny that religious
persecution existed in Cuba. As Valladares says, these
religious leaders embraced not the imprisoned Christians but their jailers and executioners. So this too is
what "never again" must mean. I am afraid that that is
a lesson from the Holocaust, and from subsequent hor-
rors, that we have still not learned very well. Never again
must we, in the name of a sentimentalized effort to
create good will or in the name of some great liberation-
ist cause, embrace the jailers and executioners of the
martyrs.

Klenicki: Yes, and I would add to that that there is a tendency among religious leaders to denounce the horror
of life under the Argentinian generals, but to keep quiet
about the Russian treatment of Poles or of Afghanistan,
or about the reality in Nicaragua and Cuba. I am much
concerned about this selective way of denouncing evil.

Neuhaus: That is very important. I think it was Stephen
Spender who, out of his experience with the Spanish
Civil War in the 1930s, criticized his friends for refusing
to condemn the atrocities of the Communists. "No criticism to the Left" was the slogan. And of course we must
also reject the slogan "No criticism to the Right."
Spender said that those who do not care about *every*
child that is killed do not really care about *any* child
that is killed. That strikes me as very wise.

But I think you will agree with me, Leon, that one
of our problems, in the Jewish-Christian dialogue as
well, is the relentless politicizing of everything. The basic
biblical beliefs and paradigms that ought to provide a
measure of unity are captured for narrowly partisan
purposes. I know that you have written about the use,

and misuse, of the Exodus account in different forms of liberation theology.

Klenicki: Yes. Some exponents of liberation theology use the book of Exodus for support, but only up to chapter 19, disregarding chapter 20, the great moment of total revelation of God on Mount Sinai. There is also no reference to the chapters that follow, which relate to the reality of the covenant in everyday life, to the ritual and spirituality of the community before reaching the Promised Land. This is a very selective way of reading Exodus. The text is used as a pretext for explaining present social problems. The theologians' main concern, which we share, is the situation of the poor. Poverty requires denunciation but it also requires solutions. The solution recommended by liberation theologians is a sort of state socialism that is already bankrupt in the world. They are critical of capitalism, though Latin America has not yet experienced this economic system. Mercantilism, the present reality, needs a process of transformation, a process that is not understood by liberation theology.

Liberation thought is not sensitive to Latin American minorities, to Protestants and Jews. Zionism is disregarded even though it is a form of liberation, the beginning of redemption, as the Chief Rabbinate has pointed out in the Israeli prayer book.

Neuhaus: You said, Leon, that in the Israeli prayer book, Israel itself, the establishment of Israel, is viewed as a redemptive event.

Klenicki: Yes. It is part of the exile-and-return process that I described before. After Auschwitz, the exile par excellence, the creation of the state of Israel is a return and an expression of hope. Sometimes I use the term "resurrection." We in the twentieth century have been resurrected. We are incorporated now in a body called the state of Israel. We are "incarnated" in the return to the Promised Land. For that reason, the rabbis are talking about Israel as the beginning of redemption.

Neuhaus: Isn't it a little odd, though? I mean, the metaphor of Israel as a kind of resurrection from the dead sounds curiously Christian.

Klenicki: No, it is Pharisaic, part of the belief of the Pharisaic movement of the first century that was taken over by the rabbis. In our daily prayers we praise God for reviving and resurrecting the dead. So it is not a Christian concept. On the contrary, Christianity has taken this concept from Pharisaic Judaism. A Jewish person feels uneasy about using the word "resurrection" because, as you said, it sounds "Christian." When I am criticized for using it, I read the text from our prayer book. The morning and afternoon prayers praise God who performs the act of resurrection.

Anti-Zionism and Anti-Semitism

Neuhaus: As you know, the subject of the state of Israel often sets off alarms in Jewish-Christian discussions. I am thinking here of Christians who are otherwise well-informed and sympathetic to the dialogue. I do not mean fringe elements who deny that the Holocaust ever happened, or who subscribe to the obscene United Nations resolution that Zionism is the same thing as racism. I have in mind responsible Christians who say that it is one thing to speak of the continuing providential relationship between Christianity and Judaism, but quite another to let the dialogue turn into a theological defense of Zionism. They are in no way prepared to say that being pro-Jewish means being pro-Zionist, or, obversely, that anti-Zionism is anti-Semitism. The familiar point is made that an important difference between Christians and Jews is that Christians cannot attribute theological status to "a piece of real estate," in this case Israel, in the way that Jews do. And, of course, this is usually combined with what they feel is a question of justice for the Arab people, especially the Palestinians. I expect this is a continuing neuralgic point between many Christians and Jews, and will continue to have an impact on the dialogue, as it has in the past.

Klenicki: I would agree with you that some anti-Zionist Christians might not be anti-Semitic. But I would point out that anti-Zionism is, nowadays, a refined form of the teaching of contempt. Essentially, it is anti-Judaism and anti-Semitism.

Neuhaus. For the sake of clarity, Leon: You are saying that on the lips of many people, anti-Zionism is in fact a form of anti-Semitism.

Klenicki: Yes . . .

Neuhaus: But you would agree that there are anti-Zionists who are not anti-Semites?

Klenicki: Yes, I would. But many times, it is very difficult to make that distinction—very, very difficult. I would point out that Zionism was not invented by Theodor Herzl at the beginning of our century; it's imbedded in the very essence of Judaism. In Genesis 12, there is the promise of the land. That land becomes meaningful throughout the biblical context: in the psalms, in our liturgy, in the Passover celebration, in the spirituality of Israel. There is a close relationship between the land and the covenant with God. We cannot separate them. It is part of our being from the very, very beginning.

Neuhaus: Perhaps we should pause here for a moment. You are saying that Zionism is not the invention of the Zionist movement of the last century and this, but is rather an integral part of Jewish existence and belief. But isn't it true that prior to the Second World War there were many Jews, perhaps a majority of Jews, who were not Zionists and indeed opposed Zionism? One thinks, for example, of major organizations such as the American Jewish Congress, if I'm not mistaken. And anti-Zionism was not and is not limited to assimilated and secularized Jews. The Hasidim of Brooklyn, for instance, and many of the super-Orthodox in Israel itself are anti-Zionist, I believe. In other words, isn't it true that, both historically and at present, substantial numbers of Jews would not say that Zionism is part and parcel of Jewish existence and belief?

Klenicki: I must disagree with you, Richard. I would say that those Jews who do not believe in Zionism are a small minority. This was not true before World War II, however. A large number of Jews in Europe hoped to be able to live their lives expressing their culture as Jews through various movements, such as the Jewish socialist movement in Poland. Non-observant Jews truly believed they could be assimilated into the societies of such enlightened countries as Germany and France. Therefore, Zionism did not play the role it does today.

History rudely awakened us from that dream of acceptance. There is a group, a very fundamentalist one, in
Jerusalem that is against the state. They feel that only
the Messiah will bring about a Jewish state. But they
are in the minority. The vast majority of Jews believe in
the existence of the state of Israel and are very concerned about its security.

Neuhaus: That is a very useful clarification, Leon. Given
everything we have said about the particularistic and
historical character of Jewish and Christian faith, it
should not surprise us that historical contingencies af-
fect our understanding of who we are and what we are
obliged to do. A post-Holocaust understanding is different from a pre-Holocaust understanding. It makes perfect sense that, in the shadow of the Shoah, many Jews
came to recognize for the first time that support for the
state of Israel is part of being Jewish. I recall Prime Min-
ister Golda Meier once making the argument in a particularly effective way: religious considerations aside, it
is impossible today to be for the Jewish people without
being for the state of Israel. The simple reality of the dis-
tribution of Jews in the world means that the future of
Living Judaism is entangled with the question of the
survival and safety and prosperity of Israel.

Klenicki: Yes. It is very important to point out that the
exercise of Judaism and the relationship with God will
have one aspect in the state of Israel and might have
other qualities in societies where we are a minority.

I would like to come back to a matter we considered
briefly before. We said before that criticism of the state
of Israel by Christians does not make them anti-Semitic.
But the tone of the criticism makes the difference. The
critique of certain groups with vested interests in the
Middle East reminds me of Christian theology's teach-

ing of contempt, which denies Judaism a role in God's plan of salvation, if I may use terminology that is familiar to you. But in the twentieth century, by denying Israel the right to defend its integrity, Christian critics are denying Israel a role in history. The ambiguity of some Christian documents on Israel and the absence of any positive reference to the Jewish state are examples of a new teaching of contempt. It is a repetition of history: we were denied theologically in the past, and we are denied ideologically today.

Neuhaus: Are you also concerned about the state of unbelief in Israel among the Jews?

Klenicki: Oh, yes, very much, and especially because it *is* in the Promised Land. Certain points of that unbelief are a reaction, a sort of anti-clericalism in reaction to the fundamentalism of certain groups in Israel, particularly among young people.

Neuhaus: Just as a parenthesis . . .

Klenicki: Yes?

Neuhaus: Maybe this will be useful, because I hope there will be some fundamentalist readers of this book. You have, throughout this conversation, used the term "fundamentalism" in referring to a certain style of Jewish teaching and piety. Is that an appropriate term to use? I mean, after all, it's a term that comes out of a peculiarly Christian—and, for the most part, American—circumstance.

Klenicki: Well, I use it in a general way, not in a Christian way, to refer to people who are ultra-fanatic in their traditional beliefs.

Neuhaus: Rather than moderately fanatic?

Klenicki: (laughs)

Neuhaus: Fine, I take the point.

Klenicki: I think I'm fanatical in my Judaism in a moderate way. I'm sensitive to a lot of people, including my fellows Jews who are not religiously inclined, as well as those who are less religiously inclined, or more religiously inclined, than I am. But it's important to point out, as I said before, that criticism of the state of Israel by certain Christians does not make such people anti-Israel or anti-Semitic. But I feel that in certain circles, there is a criticism of the state of Israel that reminds me of the teaching of contempt, the teaching of the church fathers in the Middle Ages, who denied us a place in God's plan of salvation. In the twentieth century, by denying Israel its own way and its own struggle, certain Christian thinkers and critics are denying a historical role to Israel. Some Christian denominations who recognize our place in God's design are nevertheless over-critical of Israel's actions while remaining silent about the brutal terrorism employed by Israel's enemies.

Neuhaus: So the message is that there are people who are not anti-Semites but are nonetheless, inadvertently, guilty of complicity in the teaching of contempt. But you well know that Christians have a very real problem with Israel, in that there is nothing comparable in Christian teaching with respect to the actual place, a piece of earth, on which God's purpose is contingent. Obviously, we have our holy places, chiefly in the Holy Land. But there is what some call this "universalizing thrust" in Christianity, this understanding that God is equally present to every moment and every place. So there are many Christians who insist that it is upon theological grounds that they must refuse to say about the state of Israel what many Jews want them to say. In addition, as mentioned earlier, there is the concern for the Palestinians, and then too the long history of Christian mission among Arab peoples. The Vatican, as you know, makes no secret of its anxiety about the fate of Christian communities within the Arab world. For the Vatican, as well as for other Christians, it is a matter of grave pastoral and moral responsibility, and that in large part explains the "evenhandedness" toward Israelis and Arabs that so many Jews deplore.

For all the reasons we've discussed, I believe a Christian pledge to—even a kind of covenant with—Israel is imperative. In addition, as an American citizen I am convinced that Israel is vital to the fate of democracy and freedom in the world. Of course, that is a prudential judgment and is eminently debatable—indeed, it is frequently hotly debated. But all of these issues impinge upon the dialogue. How do we respond to those Christians who say that if they say what we would like them to say about Israel, their words will be interpreted as anti-Palestinian? They are nervous, in addition, that statements favorable to Israel will be seen as a carte blanche endorsement of everything the state of Israel does or has done, some of which they believe is unconscionable.

Klenicki: I think that Christian leadership, especially Protestant churches, have an important role to play in the Middle East—not taking sides, but helping people in that area to understand each other. Some religious leaders see Palestinians—even terrorists—as victims, and Jews as the victimizers. Some Christian leaders have pointed out to me that this is a difficult matter for them. Years ago, Jews were the victims par excellence,

and now, according to them, the Jews appear as the victimizers par excellence. It should be explained and said
to the Jewish people and Israel that Christian support
of the Palestinian community does not mean support of
the PLO or any group that wants to destroy the state of
Israel. To many Jews, when Christians ask the state of
Israel to talk with the PLO and to start negotiating with
them, it sounds like a comedy of ambiguities. These
leaders are asking Israel to deal with a group who denies the existence of the state. It's like a Borges story.
But while it might be good in literature, it is totally naïve
when considering the complicated political problem of
the Middle East. It is unfair to Israel and her delicate
political situation.

I remember years ago the National Council of
Churches sent a delegation to check on human rights
in the state of Israel. It seems that they didn't discover
any lack of human rights. It would have been more appropriate to have sent a delegation to Jordan and to
Syria for that purpose. But they sent it only to Israel.
They met with Arafat and with other terrorist leaders,
but did not attempt any action to bring peace or to build
a bridge of understanding between Israelis and Arabs.

Israel is interested in finding a solution to the problems in the area. The state wants to negotiate directly
with Arab leadership as it did with Egypt. Israel is willing
to start dialogue with any Arab countries willing to recognize the sovereignty of the state of Israel. The solution
to the Palestinian situation is closely related to a peace
treaty with Jordan. It is part of the Camp David agreement. But Israel has to feel secure. Israel is not going to
give up her security for an illusion of peace which will
be the peace of death.

Neuhaus: I think I understand that. It seems to me that
Christians must be prepared to take some risks in

speaking about Israel. Obviously, anything we say could be misinterpreted by those who have the inclination to do so. And on political questions we must be very, very careful to refrain from saying "thus saith the Lord," lest we bring the word of God into disrepute. But I find it very troubling that some of our Christian brothers and sisters, and some of our churches, are not ready to make even the most nuanced statement of support for Israel. Some of us Christians are very big on "reading the signs of the times," and end up reading all sorts of things into the signs of the times; indeed, we start making up the signs of the times. It seems that some of our churches, both on the right and on the left, seem to think they can issue daily press releases on what God is going to do in the world today. That is very disturbing.

But at the same time, I find it depressing that those who say all kinds of affirmative things about our continuing relationship with Judaism on this continent are so tongue-tied with respect to Judaism on another continent. Whether we agree with its policies or not, whether it is the way we would have designed it or not, there is no blinking the fact that the state of Israel impinges powerfully upon the well-being of Judaism in our time. The hesitancy in saying that, I expect, is frequently related to a reading of the signs of the times which results in the political judgment that, since Israel is so closely associated with the United States, it must be on the wrong side of what is called the "global revolution." I'm afraid that it's this kind of political-historical reading to which affirmations about the Jewish-Christian relationship are subordinated. On this and numerous other issues, sorting out the political from the religious and theological is no easy task. But Christians have a special problem with this sorting out when it comes to the state of Israel.

Klenicki: I would say that there are two dangers, two extremes. One would be the extreme stand of not considering Israel as essential in Jewish existence. The other extreme would be to believe that the creation of the state of Israel is the prelude to a second coming of Jesus. Those two extremes are equally dangerous. The first one is part of the teaching of contempt and does not take into consideration the centrality of the return to the Promised Land, denying the Jewish people a national vocation. The second position considers the creation of Israel, the military victory of Israel as part of God's design in a sort of a holy war against the devil represented by the Soviet Union and the Communist world. I feel unhappy about this position. We have been used for other purposes. If Jews do not accept Jesus as the Christ, will our Christian friends and admirers of Israel and Zionism become anti-Zionist and anti-Semite?

I don't remember reading much in fundamentalist writings on the question of the Holocaust as part of Jewish destiny in the twentieth century. How would fundamentalists relate the Holocaust to their expectation of a second coming?

End-Time Fears, End-Time Hopes

Neuhaus: So now we have moved the conversation to dispensationalism, as it is found among most fundamentalists and many evangelical Christians. I don't think it's accurate, Leon, to say that the Holocaust plays no part in their thinking. A good many fundamentalist leaders lift up the Holocaust as an example of the vindication of the biblical promise that those who bless the

Jews will be blessed, and those who curse the Jews will be cursed. That, they say, explains the defeat of National Socialism in Germany. This sort of argument is very common in their literature.

But you raise an interesting cluster of questions. As you know, I am not a dispensationalist. My own conviction is that there is no biblical justification for most of what is said under the banner of "Bible prophecy." In the long reach of Christian history, this mode of thought is of very recent vintage, going back to John Nelson Darby (1800-1882) in England and to the Scofield Bible in American Protestantism. So, while this kind of dispensationalism is a minority position among Christians, the Christians who subscribe to it are at present very important to the support of Israel. They have their eschatological scenarios, including the battle at Armageddon, the rapture of the saints, the coming of the millennium, and so forth. The part of all this that is troubling to Jews is the part that entails the conversion of Jews to Christ. But those who advance this position say that Jews should not be troubled by that. "Look," they say, "this is the way it's going to happen, and at that point Jews will recognize that the Messiah who comes is indeed the Messiah, and the only difference between Jews and Christians is that Christians will welcome him as the Jesus who had come before." So for Christians it will be the second coming, and for Jews the first coming. Thus they insist that their position in no way constitutes a rejection of Judaism, but rather proclaims the rightness of an inherently Jewish Messianic hope.

Klenicki: But it might bring problems to both Jews and Christians. For Jews, trying to accept the Christian view that it's a second coming would require much re-thinking of past history. For Christians to recognize that for Jews it is only the first coming would bring greater trouble. The Messianic time, the coming of the Messiah, might bring some painful theological problems for both of us. Until that time, I am a firm believer that both Jews and Christians have much to do jointly for the kingdom of God, especially in the United States.

Neuhaus: I recall Rabbi Pinchas Lapide's dialogue with Karl Rahner on this matter of the end time. Lapide said, "That he will be Jesus of Nazareth is a certainty for you and a not-to-be-precluded possibility for me. No more, but also no less. So here, therefore, there is no Jewish 'no' standing over against a Christian 'yes,' but rather a Christian 'yes' to a humble Jewish question mark." I am sure we could discuss that fruitfully. But you suggest that we have to look to our common tasks in the time before the end time. In that connection, you might agree with Irving Kristol's statement about fundamentalist support for Israel: "It's their theology, but it's our Israel." He is quite ready to accept the support without getting entangled in the theology.

Klenicki: Yes. I would say yes, especially since we feel abandoned by so many Christians in days of trouble. I remember that in 1967 there were very few Christian responses of support for Israel at a moment of great danger for the security and survival of the state.

Jewish Influence

Neuhaus: Leon, I think it would be useful for us here to at least touch on another factor that has often led to misunderstanding—namely, what is often called the Jewish lobby in the United States. The Jewish or pro-Israel lobby is described as the most powerful lobby in Washington, and it is said that that accounts for the fact that the bulk of U.S. aid overseas goes to Israel. Is this question about "disproportionate Jewish influence in American foreign policy" a source of anxiety? Should it be?

Klenicki: I am concerned about the use of the expression "Jewish lobbying." It is a way of denigrating the efforts of the community to protect itself. Lobbying is a legitimate and important element in our democratic process. Beyond that, there is a tendency to overstate the influence of the Jewish community in American Middle East policy and support of Israel. U.S. aid to Israel rests primarily on factors other than the role of the Jewish community. When Richard Nixon and Jimmy Carter and Ronald Reagan dramatically increased U.S. aid to Israel and strengthened strategic relations between the two countries, the American Jewish factor was far down on the list of influences. Perceptions of Israel's role in deterring Soviet influence, the impact of a strong Israel on the peace process, and the ideological need to protect an ally and democracy dominated U.S. thinking. And in the 1980s, it was the strategic outlook of the American government together with the decline of oil influence which generated the next level of U.S. assistance to Israel. The American Jewish community has labored diligently to encourage these processes and will continue to do so. But it is an unfortunate misreading to place such heavy weight on its role.

Neuhaus: This matter of the role of Jews in American life engages our understanding of the Diaspora. Moving away from the geopolitical dimensions of this—support for Israel, and so forth—we might ask, What is the theological and spiritual significance of the Diaspora? There are more Jews outside Israel today than there are in Israel. Christians may wonder whether many of these Jews, especially the believers among them, might not have something of a guilty conscience about not living in Israel. Certainly there are many Jews who proclaim that living in Israel is the fulfillment of their Jewishness. So the questions must be asked: Is the Diaspora a second-best thing? Is the Diaspora a strategic necessity in order to sustain support for Israel in the rest of the world? Or does the Diaspora community have a spiritual status and dignity in its own right?

Klenicki: I would say that it is all of that and more. Israel needs the help of Jews outside of Israel, needs their friendship and support. But it is also true that Jews outside of Israel need Israel as our homeland and as a visible sign of God's covenant, as it was in biblical times. There were Jews who remained in Babylon and Jews who went back with Ezra and Nehemiah to Jerusalem. Both communities continued building their Jewishness. In the case of the community in the land of Israel, scholars, scribes, and commentators built Jewish life after exile through the Pharisaic revolution, while the Jews in Babylon, through the centuries, were able to codify the Babylonian Talmud. Whoever reads the pages of the Talmud will realize that you need an intelligentsia in order to prepare such a body of literature. So I wouldn't set one against the other. We are together as part of the people of God. There is the heart of Judaism which is Jerusalem, and there are also the people who are building and rebuilding the body of Judaism. We are together the "mystical body" of God's call.

Neuhaus: But if Israel is essential to the present and future well-being of Judaism, why is it not imperative for

more Jews—especially Jews of Western achievement
and affluence—to actually live there? If one looks at the
demographics, it would seem that Israel is less and less
a country of Western Europeanized Jews and is becoming more and more a Middle Eastern country in every
sense of the term. Is there not going to come a time in
which the cultural ties between Jews of the Diaspora
and the majority of Jews in Israel will become so at-
tenuated that the linkage between Israel and worldwide
Judaism will be severely weakened?

Klenicki: No, because I think that in Israel itself there is
a demographic transformation. The Western Jews and
the Oriental Jews are mingling together, especially in
the army, where they learn to be Israelis, beyond different origins. Also, since Israel is a democracy, minorities
change and adapt, just as minorities in American life
do. The same occurs in Israel. For example, the Sephar-
dim, who are Jews from Arab countries or Arab Jews,
and the Jews from Western societies each stress ties to
their own cultures for a time, but after a generation they
become totally Israeli.

The Israeli Jew is becoming a very special product
of his land. He is called "Sabra," the fruit of a cactus, an
image which portrays the native Jew very well, since the
sabra is very tough outside but sweet inside. Jewish individuals in the Promised Land develop with different
pressures and different understandings of their socio-
logical and historical situation. The fact that they are
surrounded by a hostile Arab world means that the
Israelis have to defend themselves. It is a question of
survival. The Israeli is becoming a special kind of Jew.

We share some problems. We in the West are surrounded by a non-Jewish world, and we are suffering
the constant seduction of the Western culture that is in-
viting us to give up our values and our beliefs. Some-

thing similar is occurring in Israel, where there is a new generation with a weak background in Judaism as a way of thinking and living. They have lots of Israelism, but not necessarily the Judaism of tradition. This is a very complex problem that is affecting the new generation, both here in America and in Israel. There is also the problem of trying to respond to the question of how to be a Jew at the end of the twentieth century, both inside and outside of Israel. It goes back to what I said before: the challenge of the Holocaust is how to build and rebuild the inner temple. But it is important to stress that Israelis also need to defend their right to be an independent nation. This must not be forgotten by any of us, Christians or Jews.

One interesting development in Israel is that some collective farms, called kibbutzim, especially socialist kibbutzim, are becoming more and more interested in theological matters. There are some promising religious programs in cooperation with the Reform movement, a unique contribution to Israeli spirituality.

Neuhaus: Have you ever seriously considered living in Israel?

Klenicki: Yes, I have thought about that very much. I feel that my covenantal relationship requires that culmination: to live in the land, the space given by God in his promise and call to Abraham. However, my work brought me to America, and here, because of the unique pluralism of our democracy, I have been able to experience spiritual integrity living as a Jew.

Neuhaus: And that is a very American way of viewing the matter. This leads me to think that we might explore, at least a little, some of the questions surrounding cultural assimilation. Under the European system of toleration, for example, many Jews faded into the cultural wood-work, so to speak. This does not mean that they neces-sarily converted, although many did, but anything that stuck out as Jewish was carefully tucked back in so that it would not be noticeable.

Klenicki: Yes. One became German on the street, a Jew at home.

A Consistent Life Ethic

Neuhaus: Right. And it is, in retrospect, astonishing to recognize the degree to which Jews felt secure in that context. We know from the literature that in Germany, right up to the implementation of "the final solution," many Jews simply refused to believe what was happen-ing. They were confident that they were Germans first, that they truly belonged to this national community, and they found it impossible to accept the fact that Ger-many turned out to be so dramatically different from the Germany they had embraced and called their own.

Now we must certainly be careful in drawing his-torical analogies, but there are ominous ways in which the ugly face of barbarity seems to be appearing in American life. Of course this is not—and is not going to become—Nazi Germany. Whatever happens here will, for better or worse, be very American. But I am think-ing, for example, of developments surrounding repro-ductive technology, genetic engineering, the farming and harvesting of fetuses for experimental and trans-plant purposes, and the powerful push in favor of euthanasia. In short, we are witnessing, I believe, the return of eugenics, the attempt to assert complete technological control over the human condition. It may turn out that the Nazi experience simply induced a momentary pause in the inexorable advance of eugenic ideology and practice. Today, for instance, the proponents of these developments use "quality of life" indexes, indexes which are substantially identical to the Nazi doctrine of *lebensunwertes Leben*, life that is not worthy of life. You are well aware of the Vatican "Instruction" of 1987, which very forcefully spoke to some of these developments. Many other Christians have also raised an alarm. In this connection a frequent puzzlement is expressed about the relative quiet of the Jewish community on these issues, with the exception of Orthodox Judaism. But what some view as the Jewish mainline— some of the major organizations, for instance—seems to be reluctant to address questions which, in view of the Holocaust, one might think Jews would be the first to address.

Klenicki: I would distinguish between our religious organizations and those organizations in our community whose task is to defend the Jewish people in the fight against anti-Semitism. I would say that our more traditional religious organizations have paid a lot of attention to the developments you mentioned and have issued statements and studies on these matters. The Reform movement, which is more interested in social issues, has lately expressed concern about biological engineering and related matters.

I, personally, would not like to make a religious crusade of the criticism of biological engineering. As a religious person, I care about those aspects of technology that are becoming ideologies, ends in themselves, and which oppose my basic belief as a person of God.

But that does not mean that I have to join a crusade, such as the anti-alcohol crusade in the 1900s. I want to make that distinction because otherwise we might confuse matters. Not everything is evil in the new technology. We have made positive contributions to life.

Neuhaus: But Leon, why not a crusade? I mean, if the sacredness of human life and the sustaining of a civilized community of concern for the marginal and vulnerable is at stake—while I don't particularly care for the word "crusade"—if there is anything worth crusading about, why isn't this it?

Klenicki: Let's clarify what we are crusading for. If, for example, a woman declares in her last will that she does not want to prolong her life if she will be in a state of coma, I think we should follow her will and decision.

Neuhaus: There is widespread agreement, also grounded in Christian and Jewish ethics, about not using "extraordinary means" to prolong life when they would be excessively burdensome or counterproductive. As you know, there is a great deal of literature on that subject. But what we're talking about now, and what is actually being done, is the withdrawal of food and water in order to terminate life. And this is done not only to the comatose or to people in the last stage of dying, but it is also done to people who have no say in the matter, people who are killed because somebody else decides that it is in their "best interest" to live no longer. The deliberate starvation of handicapped children, for example, has been upheld by courts in several states. And in state legislatures, backed by a massive media blitz, we have bills allowing measures such as "assisted suicide" and the taking of body parts from human beings who are declared to be dead before they really are. In short, we're talking about much more than the use of extraordinary means to sustain life.

Klenicki: Yes, I would be against all those measures. Many in the Jewish community would be against them. There are sound Halakic rules for opposing those measures, as well as a respect for human life. But I want to say it again: I do not want to make a crusade out of that and disregard other problems. I do not want an ideology of anti-science that will take us back a century.

Neuhaus: Agreed, we should not disregard other problems. But there are few other problems as monumental as the threat posed by these developments. And again, we're not speaking here of things that might happen in the future, but of things that are happening now, and of other measures being pushed in the public arena. We don't have to be—and shouldn't be—alarmist about these matters; just thinking about them clearly is alarming enough. The point I would raise is that, while many Jews have been involved in the pro-life movement for a long time, the Jewish presence is not nearly so prominent in this movement as it is in groups such as Planned Parenthood, the American Civil Liberties Union, and other organizations that pro-lifers view as being on the pro-death side of these issues. Does this not strike you as strange and ominous, precisely in the light of everything we've said about the Holocaust?

Klenicki: Well, here I would like to stress my great discomfort with what you just said in linking abortion with the Holocaust. This has also been done by certain Catholic leaders. I want to point out that during the Holocaust, there was no choice for abortion or no abortion. Girls were raped and were later sent to the gas chambers. In the United States, a woman has several choices.

She can have an abortion—which I consider an immoral act—or she can give birth and give the child up for adoption, or she can ask for help from other sources. But she is not without choices as Jewish women were in the Holocaust. There was no way out under the Nazis. In America, there are other ways out.

Neuhaus: Well, I agree with you that one must be very careful in drawing any historical analogies or parallels, especially when the subject at hand is as ominous as the Holocaust. At the same time, on the question of not having a choice, the point of analogy here is that the unborn child also does not have a choice.

Klenicki: Yes, but according to rabbinic theology, the fetus is an individual living organism only at the time of birth. This is the rabbinic rule. While the fetus remains inside the mother, it is only a part of the mother.

Neuhaus: Oh, but surely there are Jewish authorities who have written quite to the contrary, that the Jewish position is almost identical with that of those Christians who believe that it is at the point of conception that the new creation has taken place which must be respected as a member of the human community.

Klenicki: Well, I would say also that in Judaism, we don't have a magisterium, as in the Catholic church. We have different opinions. If you read the text from the Mishnah, you will find different opinions about the same problems. So I can go through my tradition and show all sorts of cases for the possibility of abortion, and also many against any form of abortion.

Neuhaus: Okay, so let's stipulate that there are disagreements in the Jewish community as to what Halakic tradition says about this. But surely, should it not bother more Jews than it evidently does that a court can make discriminations as to what constitutes human life in the full sense of the word, as in the case of Roe v. Wade, and can exclude from communal protections those who, presumably because they are not "viable," have no claim upon the community's protection? There are many people who would say that many individuals—the so-called "vegetables" in our state hospitals, the handicapped, the mentally ill, the "useless aged"—that all of these people are not human beings in the full sense of the word. Doesn't this logic itself, quite apart from the specific policy applications, set off alarm bells in the Jewish heart?

Klenicki: Getting back to what I was just saying, I would like to stress woman's responsibility for her own body. Even if a fetus is only an appendage until birth, a woman should be respectful of it as she should be of any part of her body. She should be even more respectful of it since it is the part of her body that will become a person after birth.

Neuhaus: But, Leon, surely a fetus is a different case altogether. No other "appendage" has the potential of becoming another human being, even if if were permitted to do so. Perhaps responsibility toward one's body parts is irrelevant here.

Klenicki: No, I don't think so. I think we should analyze that. Personally, I feel horrified by the popularity of the abortion movement because in certain respects it shows a lack of responsibility on the part of both women and men in creating life that they were not planning to create. And this serious lack of responsibility also shows a lack of responsibility to society itself, a tendency which has been growing in the United States in the last twenty years.

But there can also be special cases in which an abortion may be justified—for example, a hereditary disease, measles, or other problems that can make a woman seriously concerned about the condition of her child after birth. In that case, the rabbis are open to such an operation before the baby is born.

Neuhaus: But we have agreed that many Jewish authorities would challenge your interpretation.

Klenicki: Yes, exactly. And that is a sign of the pluralism of our community.

The State of Anti-Semitism

Neuhaus: Maybe we can move on to some more general questions about the way in which the Jewish community understands itself in the American context, and specifically about the state of anti-Semitism in America. As you know, there are a number of themes that recur again and again in classical anti-Semitism. Two prominent, and mutually contradictory, ones are, first, that Jews are at the heart of the capitalist conspiracy, and second, that they are at the heart of the conspiracy to overthrow capitalism. That is, it is said that "international Jewry" pulls all the money strings, thus controlling capitalism here and around the world. At the same time, anti-Semites tell us that Jews are running the international Marxist conspiracy aimed at the revolutionary overthrow of capitalism. These and other themes of anti-Semitism are very marginal in America, appearing only in the fever swamps of the political right and left. And this undoubtedly has much to do with the fact that Jews feel "at home" in America, probably more than in any other place or at any other time in the last two millennia, except for Israel. Anti-Semitism, while always a cause for concern, does not have the deep cultural roots here that it has in some European societies, for instance. You can see that I'm trying to get you to say something about the studies done by your organization, the Anti-Defamation League of B'nai B'rith— studies that show not only a remarkably low level of anti-Semitism in America but also, on the part of the overwhelming majority of Americans, a very positive attitude toward Jews and Judaism.

Klenicki: Yes, and in that respect I would like to refer to two studies developed by the Anti-Defamation League of B'nai B'rith in the last twenty-five years. In the sixties we did a joint study with the University of California called "Christian Beliefs and Anti-Semitism" under the directorship of Charles Glock and Rodney Stark, under the supervision of Oscar Cohen (ADL), a pioneer in fostering dialogue. Through this study of religious Christian texts and their presentation of Jews and Judaism, we realized that the teaching of contempt was still rampant and that it required an interreligious consideration. This was done through a study of catechetical materials. Publishers followed up on the research in revising the textbooks. I would say that now practically no Catholic text has negative references to Jews and Judaism. Recently a Catholic publisher issued a set of guidelines, *Within Context,* on the presentation of Jews and Judaism in the teaching of the New Testament, prepared by a group of rabbinic and

New Testament scholars under the directorship of the National Conference of Catholic Bishops and ADL.

ADL has done a similar study among evangelicals on this subject, but it is simpler and less academic than the California study. We studied the reactions of the evangelical community vis-à-vis Judaism, the Jewish people, and the state of Israel, and we made some surprising discoveries. In general, the Jewish community expects a sort of anti-Judaism in the evangelical community, though they are great supporters of the state of Israel.

Neuhaus: The Glock-Stark study in the 1960s reinforced the assumption that the more conservative or orthodox Christians are, the more likely it is that they will be anti-Semitic. But now this more recent study, as you say, tends to challenge that assumption.

Klenicki: Yes, it does. We found that there is a better understanding of Jews and Judaism in the evangelical community. But there is, of course, a difference of twenty-five years between our first study and the present one. Many things have changed in American society during this period.

Evangelical denunciation of anti-Semitism was evident at the showing of *The Last Temptation of Christ*. The National Association of Evangelicals criticized fundamentalist groups that expressed anti-Semitism in attacking the movie studios and their officials. Some of those officials are Jewish, and the film appeared, according to some fundamentalist critics, as a "Jewish conspiracy to crucify Jesus for the second time." The text of the film was criticized as a pretext to reveal what is still in the minds of many fundamentalists—the anti-Semitism created by the teaching of contempt.

Evangelicals are critical of their own people when they express anti-Jewish remarks. In the case of Bailey

Smith, who said that God doesn't hear the prayer of the Jews, for example, a majority of the people who answered the ADL's poll criticized Rev. Smith and resented such an expression of contempt for the Jewish people.

Neuhaus: The controversy surrounding the Bailey Smith statement was a curious one, but not as curious as the statement itself. From a Christian viewpoint, it is ludicrous to suggest that an omniscient and merciful God does not hear the prayers, or any other word, from his entire creation. Jesus has told us that the Father has counted every hair on our heads and that he takes note of every sound uttered by his groaning creation, as Saint Paul describes it.

But there is something else in play here as well. Christians like Bailey Smith are prompted by the desire to express the singularity of the relationship established with God through Christ. Sometimes they do this in a way that violates the civil protocols of a pluralistic society, and also, more importantly, in a way that violates the divinely ordained relationship between Christians and Jews. Now we have, in a sense, come full circle in our conversation, since we are back to—among other things—the question of conversion. But we should pause for a moment at this issue of civil protocols. John Murray Cuddihy, as you will recall, makes a rather eccentric but very incisive argument in his book *No Offense: Civil Religion and Protestant Taste.* He argues that many Jews and Christians in America—at least those who are in the cultural elite and who belong to what is called the new knowledge class—have come to certain understandings. They have agreed to an etiquette, a certain set of "Protestant" manners, in which they will not make particularistic truth claims which might make others uncomfortable. At least, they will not make such claims in public. With this line of thinking, civility becomes a powerfully inhibiting factor in the relationship between Jews and Christians. Our mutual perceptions are skewed as a consequence of a false politeness.

But the conversation which you and I are having is not primarily attuned to the rules of etiquette, Protestant or otherwise. Civility is important, to be sure, but it is far more important to engage one another, especially at points of significant difference. We cannot be inhibited by the fact that, at times, one party's truth may be abrasive to the other party. Giving offense, to use Cuddihy's term, is not necessarily a sign that someone has broken the rules of the conversation, but rather it can be a sign that we have touched on something that calls for further and deeper dialogue.

Klenicki: Yes, I agree with that. In that respect, it is very important that the people in dialogue should begin in faith, as Heschel pointed out. We are at a point in our historical development in the United States when inter-religious relationships require a new depth of reflection in faith, a responding together to God's call. It is a moment of sharing spiritualities respectful of differences. The American experience allows for that. It is a unique testimony of faith for the world.

Especially now, as we celebrate the two-hundredth anniversary of our Constitution, we need to reflect on the role of religion in American life, going beyond the question of separation of church and state, which at times becomes a confrontation. We need to reflect respectfully on differences in religious life in "the naked public square."

Each in the Sight of the Other in the Sight of God

Neuhaus: We can readily agree on that. Now I wonder, Leon, since we're entering the final phase of this conversation, if we should not say something more about the possibility of a more theological or more spiritual understanding of the Jewish-Christian connection. How does a believing Jew today understand Christianity within the framework of belief, and, likewise, can Christians develop a fuller view of the theological and spiritual significance of Judaism? Put differently, what does it mean for Jews to have a theology of Christianity, and for Christians to have a theology of Judaism?

Over the years I have encountered a powerful Jewish nervousness about that kind of question. I have been told by Jews, for instance, that "We do not want to be part of your theological system." And no doubt some Christians might respond in the same way, that they do not want to be part of a Jewish theological system. But I don't think that Christians actually do respond in this way, and one reason for this is the dramatic asymmetry in the cultural and demographic situation of Christians and Jews. Obviously, Christians do not feel threatened by Jews in the way that many Jews feel threatened by Christians. It has become very clear to me that many Christians quite entirely fail to understand the legitimate anxieties that Jews have with respect to their historical circumstance of being a very small minority in a pervasively, and sometimes assertively, Christian population.

There are many problems involved in talking about a Christian theology of Judaism. But all the same, I am convinced that the position of Living Judaism is not se-cure—not really secure—in this society, unless it is se-cured at the level of the ultimate beliefs, the theology, of Christians. To the extent that it is only a matter of enhancing pluralism, of not giving offense, of good in-tergroup relations, the relationship between Christian and Jew will always be fragile. I have to say quickly that one's interest in such a theological construction cannot be because of its utilitarian value in securing Jewish-Christian relations. In other words, it may be a "useful" construction but, if it is not warranted by revelation, it cannot be accepted as true.

I am convinced that Christian respect—even rever-ence—for Living Judaism is not only theologically war-ranted but is also mandated by the biblical witness. The continuing history of Judaism is not simply a theolog-ical anomaly. It is, if we accept what Paul says, a mys-tery before which we must bow our heads. We must also bow our heads in the sense that we are not capable of comprehending precisely what are God's intentions in this history in which we are both participants. Failing to reverence that mystery can lead to great danger for Jews in a majority Christian society, as we have dis-cussed. But there is also a great danger, a spiritual danger, for Christians. If Christians turn against Judaism, they are turning against the very story of sal-vation on which their own existence depends. They are turning against Christ. But this spiritual and theolog-ical understanding of our relationship is in some ways only just beginning, isn't it?

Klenicki: Right.

Neuhaus: And yet, while "theology" is not, as you say, a Jewish term, certainly "belief" is. Whether one uses the term "theology" or "religious philosophy" or "belief" or

"spirituality," the subject involves truth claims about reality and its ultimate meaning. And that is what we call
theology. Of course, theology can be understood as an
elitist enterprise that is limited to certified theologians.
But in this connection I understand theology as faith
and piety and practice. I would like to think that we are
on the edge of a time in which Judaism will have an important place in the understanding of the Christian
people, in the *sensus fidelium*. That time has not yet
come; we should not fool ourselves about that. Many
Christians—I expect even most Christians—can readily
say, "Well, I know he's Jewish, but it's all right, it doesn't
make any difference." That is simply the level of toleration, as we discussed earlier. And of course toleration is
to be desired if the only alternative is religious warfare.
But the much-more-to-be-desired alternative is a
deeper fellowship and respect for each other, and a
shared understanding of God's purposes. For the Christian, it *should* make a difference that someone is a Jew.

Klenicki: Yes. And I would say that this must begin with
security. For us Jews, security is central and urgent.
When we feel secure, we can relate to other religious
people and understand their mission, their message to
the world. I would say that two thousand years ago, we
felt secure despite being under Roman rule. Because we
felt secure, we were able to produce a document like the
Avodah Zarah, a critical appraisal of pagan religions and
Gnosticism. But for centuries after that, we were not
able to reflect on other religious creeds, particularly
Christianity, because of Christian authoritarianism. It
is only now, in the pluralistic security of the U.S.A., that
there are again Jewish attempts to reflect on and understand the meaning and mission of Christianity.

We must start to try to understand Christianity and
the mission of Christianity. I do not like to use the

expression "a Jewish theology of Christianity." "Theology" is not our term for this. Often when we use the term "theology," we are thinking of the word *Halakah*, which can be translated as "spirituality"—that is, the implementation of God's command in our lives. In the exercise of our spirituality we have to reflect on the meaning of Christianity. Not in the sense of copying methods of the Christian's way, but in the sense of trying to understand that in this society, both Jews and Christians—we the minority, Christians the majority—have a mission to witness God's presence. We Jews have to learn about Christianity, getting beyond memories, beyond feelings that might easily become prejudice, and Christians have a similar task after two thousand years of contempt and triumphalism. It is not easy for any one of us. But being religious is never an easy task. God asks much of us.

Neuhaus: And so we come back to the insight that it is at points of difference that we discover our deeper unity. We, Christians and Jews, are locked in dialogue, sometimes locked in argument, and there's no getting out of it without running away from the God who has thrown us together.

As we come to the end of this conversation, I can see that we have discussed many points of difference, some of them differences between Jews and Christians, and perhaps some of them just differences between us as individuals. Even if we had all the time in the world, we could not resolve all of these differences. The ultimate difference will be resolved—one way or another, and probably in a way that will surprise all of us—only in the end time, in the Messianic Age, the kingdom of God. The Christian's highest allegiance must be to the gospel, to the piety and faith of the church. There are aspects of the gospel that the Christian cannot trim or adjust in order to make our belief less troubling to Jewish brothers and sisters. But, at the same time, it is nothing less than the gospel that opens us to Judaism and makes the dialogue imperative.

Similarly, as a believing Jew, there are things that you must say, questions you must ask, challenges that you must pose, because you are a Jew, and for some Christians these may give offense. But such moments of difference do not indicate points at which the conversation stops, but rather they are precisely the points at which the conversation must be renewed and deepened. And that kind of open-ended dialogue, that walking together, is a form of faith. And so I keep returning to Heschel's statement that "interfaith dialogue begins with faith," and that faith involves the recognition that this dialogue is not simply our doing but, much more importantly, is God's doing. Trusting him, we really do not know and do not need to know precisely how it is all going to turn out. It is enough to know that he has not and will not break his word of the covenant. I think T. S. Eliot put it just right: "For us, there is only the trying. The rest is not our business."

Klenicki: In that spirit, I would like to end our dialogue with a prayer. Prayer is essential in our relationship with God and in our own relationship as Jews and Christians. I want to quote a prayer from the morning service of the Union Prayer Book:

> May the time not be distant, O God, when your Name shall be worshipped in all the earth, when unbelief shall disappear, and error be no more. We fervently pray that the day may come when all human beings shall invoke your Name, when corruption and evil shall give way to purity and goodness, when superstition shall no longer en-

slave the mind, no idolatry blind the eye, when all who dwell on earth shall know that to you alone every knee must bend and every tongue give homage. O, may all created in your image recognize that they are brothers and sisters so that, one in spirit and one in fellowship, they may be forever united before you. Then shall your kingdom be established on earth and the word of your ancient seer be fulfilled: God will reign for ever and ever. And on that day God shall be One and his Name shall be One.

This is my great hope for our Jewish-Christian dialogue.

Neuhaus: Amen.